THE LOIRE

James Bentley

THE LOIRE

Photography by Charlie Waite

GEORGE PHILIP

British Library Cataloguing in Publication Data
Bentley, James, *1937—*
The Loire.
1. Loire River Valley (France) ——
Description and travel —— Guide-books
I. Title
914.4'504838   DC611.L81

ISBN 0-540-01105-3

Text © James Bentley 1986
Photographs © Charlie Waite 1986

First published by George Philip,
59 Grosvenor Street, London W1X 9DA

Reprinted 1989, 1991

Printed in Italy

Contents

For Emma-Jane and Ruth,
who patiently explored the Loire valley with me
even when they had important assignations elsewhere in France.

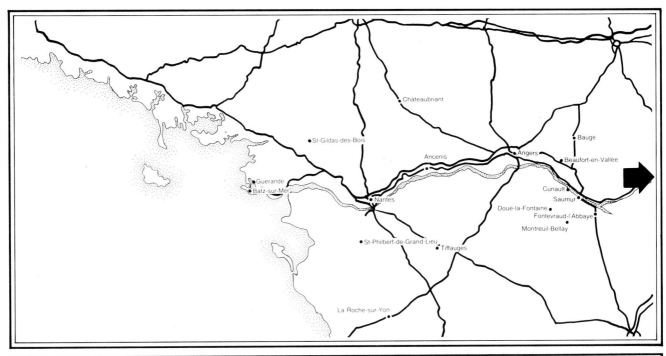

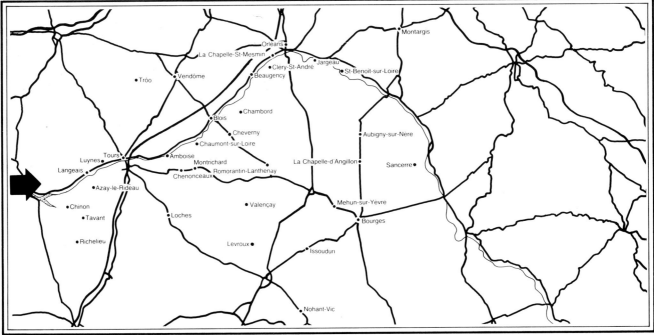

Introduction

For most of us the Loire is summed up in a eulogy by Oscar Wilde: 'One of the most wonderful rivers in the world, mirroring from sea to source a hundred cities and five hundred towers.' Our vision of the Loire valley is an extension of this – superb châteaux, ancient churches, wine and food, royal connections, natural parks and rich forests.

The River Loire is by no means the only stream to water the rich towns and valleys, and almost everywhere rivulets and torrents enhance the landscape. When Victor Hugo arrived at Blois as a young man, he was at first put off by the old dark streets. The river changed his mind. A few days later he was writing, 'I am in the most lovely town you can imagine. The way both banks of the beautiful Loire are lined is a delight to the eye: on the one side, an amphitheatre of gardens and ruins; on the other, a plain drowned in verdure.'

Two English kings and queens lie buried here. Add to this great women: Joan of Arc, Diane de Poitiers, Agnès Sorel, George Sand; troglodytes and hermits; poets such as Joachim du Bellay, Villon and Ronsard; novelists of the stature of Balzac and Alain-Fournier; ferocious noblemen like Foulques Nerra and Gilles de Retz; mystics such as Charles Péguy and Mme Guyon;

and unscrupulous or traduced clerics like Cardinal Richelieu and Urbain Grandier, and the region becomes peopled with entrancing ghosts whose spirits once responded to its charm.

The Loire is the longest river in France, rising in the Cévennes and flowing for 1020 kilometres to the Atlantic. But traditionally the region known as the Loire valley includes much more than just the valley of the river. This book describes eight modern French *départements* surrounding the great river itself (Cher, Indre, Indre-et-Loire, Loir-et-Cher, Loire-Atlantique, Loiret, Maine-et-Loire and Vendée).

The *départements* of modern France were set up only in 1790, and these eight embrace historic parts of the country more famous under other names, in particular Anjou, Berry and Brittany. Ancient Anjou took in what is now the western part of Maine-et-Loire. Its counts were some of the most powerful of France. Among them was the redoubtable Foulques Nerra, who ruled from 987 to his death in 1040. Foulques was one of the first rulers to build castles in stone rather than wood, and the Loire valley is dotted with many with which he defended his territory and acquisitions. A pious man, who founded abbeys and monasteries, he was also hot tempered and violent. Some alleged that

Left **The ample, generous River Loire, west of Amboise.**

Above **A town on the River Cher: Saint-Aignan, with its ancient church, its château, and a lovely bridge across the river.**

11

he put his first wife to death, suspecting her of adultery. To expiate his crimes he made no fewer than three pilgrimages to the Holy Land, dying at the age of seventy-two on his way back from the last.

The counts of Anjou became dukes in 1360. This great Angevin dynasty supplied not only the royal house of France but also the kings of England (who are frequently called Plantagenets) from 1154 to 1485. At times Anjou was linked directly to the French kingdom; at other times it was the hegemony of separate princes. Its last separate ruler was René I, who died in 1480, when Anjou finally reverted to the Crown of France.

The old province of Berry embraced both modern Cher and Indre. The viscounts of Berry were usually loyal and often related to the French monarchy. The

Humble architectural heritage: the so-called Mill of Balzac, in the valley of the River Indre at Pont-de-Ruan.

English coveted and fought over Berry. Jean de France, brother of the French king, became duke in the second half of the fourteenth century and managed to bring about a temporary peace between the French and English. He was less successful with his own peasants, who were so savagely taxed that they revolted in the 1380s. Jean de France exhausted his own colossal fortune, chiefly on the arts (he commissioned the Limburg brothers to produce the famous illuminated manuscript known as the *Très Riches Heures du duc de Berry*), and when he died the cash ran out before his funeral was paid for.

By contrast with Anjou and Berry, Brittany long remained obstinately outside the sway of the French kings. Independence had been achieved after a ninth-century revolt led by a warrior named Nomenoë. Nomenoë conquered both Rennes and Nantes, and for the next six centuries Brittany – often contested by the English – was ruled by dukes based on Rennes. In 1488 François II of Brittany died, leaving his lands to his daughter Anne. Her marriage to two French kings, Charles VIII and then his son Louis XII, was a major step towards uniting Brittany with the kingdom of France, a union finally secured by a treaty of 1532, when Anne of Brittany's daughter Claude sat on the throne of France as consort of François I.

For many years the kings of France preferred to live in the Loire valley rather than in Paris, basing their courts at Tours, Blois, or Amboise. Charles VII, for instance, had been King of Bourges before mounting the French throne, and he continued to live in his châteaux here, either at Bourges, or Tours, or at other sites along the banks of the river.

The Loire valley has experienced turbulence as well as years of peace and plenty. The Gauls, a Celtic tribe, migrated here from the Rhine valley in the second millennium before Christ. Their monuments still survive, especially the tall upright stones known as menhirs, and those horizontal stones resting on upright ones which are called dolmens. The Loire

Above **At Le Croisic the nineteenth-century market sells not only fish but also sacks of salt, from nearby Brittany salt-pans.**

valley was wrested from the Gauls by Julius Caesar, who defeated the famous Gaulish leader Vercingetorix in 52 BC. The Romans too left their monuments behind. When they withdrew from the region in the fifth century, Christianity had come to the Loire valley. The Franks occupied the lands north of the River Loire, the Visigoths the south. Clovis, king of the Franks, was baptised a Christian, and for a time united much of the land; but only with the accession of Charlemagne (768–814) was the kingdom fully secure. On his death his empire began to break up again.

In 1152 Eleanor of Aquitaine's marriage to King Louis VII of France was annulled and she married the future Henry II of England. Her dowry – the whole of Aquitaine – led the English kings to claim the Loire valley (and much of the rest of France) as their own.

The struggle led to what is generally known as the Hundred Years War (though it began in 1337 and did not end till 1453). Writing of the Loire valley during this unhappy time, one fifteenth-century chronicler described 'the lamentable spectacle of scattered, smoking ruins . . ., the nettles and thistles springing up on every side'. By the end of the war the English had lost all their French possessions, save for the town of Calais (which they held onto until 1558). They had also burned as a heretic the French national saint, Joan of Arc.

Firmly in power, the French monarchs soon turned to other military adventures. Charles VIII entered Italy in 1494 to assert his claim to the kingdom of Naples. For the first quarter of the sixteenth century the French owned Milan. François I campaigned in Italy in 1515 and 1516. He also fought a savage and lengthy

Below **A tiny, charming renaissance window in the formidable château at Loches.**

13

series of wars against the Holy Roman Emperor, almost losing half his kingdom in the process.

François died in 1547. During his long reign, protestantism spread into France, provoking the vicious Wars of Religion. These culminated in the massacre of 3000 protestants (Huguenots) in Paris on the eve of St Bartholomew's Day, 1572. As we shall see, the Huguenots of the Loire valley took a savage revenge. When the protestant Henri of Navarre became King Henri IV in 1589, he converted to catholicism for the sake of peace, while granting toleration to protestants by an edict proclaimed at Nantes in 1598. Toleration held until Louis XIV revoked the Edict of Nantes in 1685. In the meantime a series of brilliant, though sometimes ruthless ministers, such as Cardinal Richelieu and Louis XIV's finance minister Jean-Baptiste Colbert, brought peace and greater prosperity to the Loire valley.

The French Revolution of 1789 brought chaos. In one part of the Loire valley, the Vendée (comprising much of Loire-Atlantique and Maine-et-Loire), a massive and bloody counter-revolutionary insurrection lasted from 1793 to 1796. In Vendôme, on the other hand, the 'Conspiracy of the Equals' asserted that the Revolution had not gone far enough. Led by François-Noël ('Gracchus') Babeuf, who called himself the tribune of the people, they demanded the total abolition of private property and complete egalitarianism. The religious orders were abolished, and monasteries and abbey churches abandoned throughout the region. De-Christianization, which began in 1793 with the official declaration that communes could abandon catholic worship, led to the neglect or even mutilation of more fine churches. Tranquillity

The richness of the sixteenth century: a half-timbered house at Aubigny-sur-Nère, for many years the domain of the exiled Stuarts.

Stone owls perch and brood on the turbulent past, at Denée, near Angers.

returned only with the rule of Napoleon, who built himself a new town here to keep the Vendée in order.

The Franco-Prussian War of 1870–1, World War I and World War II all affected the Loire valley, as we shall see. And yet throughout the many disasters of the centuries, much of the precious architectural heritage of this land was retained. The Loire valley contains the oldest existing church in France, built while Charlemagne was still alive. (His palace at Aix-la-Chapelle inspired a new flowering of architecture which we now call Carolingian.) From the tenth century monks were erecting beautiful churches here in the romanesque style, usually huge halls with round arches and roofs arched like great tunnels.

Some churches were still being built in this style in the thirteenth century, but by now the people of the Loire valley were also experimenting with the pointed

15

The church of the old commune of Villeloin, at Villeloin-Coulangé, east of Montrésor. Note the decorative windows of the ancient round apse.

arches of the gothic. By the end of the twelfth century crockets and flying buttresses were appearing on these buildings, as the transition began to the French high gothic style. Anjou developed a gothic that was higher, more convex in shape than any other in France, and this graceful Angevin gothic spread throughout the region and became more and more refined. Finally, around 1375, the gothic of the Loire valley, seen at its greatest in the church of Holy Trinity, Vendôme, produced such flame-like tracery that it has become technically known as flamboyant. The house of Jacques Cœur at Bourges is the finest flamboyant palace in France.

The Italian adventures of the French kings meant that the Italian renaissance style caught the eye of the nobility. They brought back with them Italian architects, and since the court of François I was at this time at Tours, the Loire valley is the home of the finest early renaissance architecture in France. You can see the change at Blois. Louis XII built a wing between 1498 and 1503 in the flamboyant style. François I built another between 1515 and 1524, ornamented with all the devices of the Italian renaissance: square columns, double arcades, balconies, an octagonal staircase. The architect was an Italian, Domenico da Cortona, who also designed the king's stupendous renaissance château at Chambord.

The seventeenth century saw the importation of the classical style into the Loire valley. Domes, massive pillars and gables now put in their appearance, designed by architects of the calibre of François Mansart (who added a third wing to the château at Blois in 1635) and – later in the seventeenth century – J. Hardouin-Mansart.

These men designed châteaux and churches alike. Château ought not to be translated 'castle', since, strictly speaking, it means the seat of a gentleman (as opposed to château-fort, which means castle). The two definitions merge when great men and women began transforming châteaux-forts into their country houses. Early military castles consisted initially simply of a keep, the early ones square, later ones oblong and then rounded. The major change in the design of these châteaux came at the end of the thirteenth century, when crusaders brought eastern ideas of long defensive curtain walls, bolstered by many powerful towers, back to France.

The twelfth-century doorway of the cathedral at Angers. Jesus sits among the symbols of the evangelists: St Mark as a lion, St Matthew as a bull, St John as an eagle, St Luke in human form. The panels of the doors date from the seventeenth century.

This then, in brief, is an account of the history and architecture of the Loire valley. Each chapter of my book explores an area of this magical part of France, all of them centred on a great city: Nantes, Angers, Tours, Blois, Orléans and Bourges. After describing each city, I take a tour of the surrounding region. Although I do not expect that my readers will slavishly follow each route, the tours actually work. I have traversed them many times.

Arthur Young in 1792 wrote that the Loire, from Angers to Nantes, is probably 'one of the finest rivers in the world, the breadth of the stream, the islands of woods, the boldness, culture, and richness of the coast, all conspire, with the animation derived from the swelling canvas of active commerce, to render that line eminently beautiful'. Young's words apply perfectly well to the whole region.

The stunning set-pieces of the Loire valley, Château Chambord, Chenonceaux, Azay-le-Rideau and the rest, are well known. I also wish to reveal its many other charms. 'Imagine,' wrote Balzac of his own part of this entrancing country, 'three water-mills, set among gracefully chiselled islets crowned with a few clumps of trees, amid a water-meadow – what other name can one give to that aquatic vegetation, so hardy and bright, which carpets the river, undulates with it, yields to its whims and bends to the storm-waves lashed by the mill-wheels.' These gentler, lesser-known treasures of the Loire valley are as essential to my book as the greatest of its châteaux.

One last point: I have tried to indicate where places are open to the general public, sometimes even giving details of the times of opening. But these do vary. Always check at the many extremely helpful information offices (known as *Syndicats d'Initiative*).

Left **Château Chambord, redolent of royal hunts, balls, a charmed life; the architecture of fantasy.**

Below **The Loire valley is a region of exquisite details – as, for instance, this beautiful roundel in the flamboyant Château de Meillant, due north of Saint-Amand-Montrond.**

Among many others my thanks are particularly due to Mrs Pauline Hallam, public relations director of the French Government Tourist Office in London.

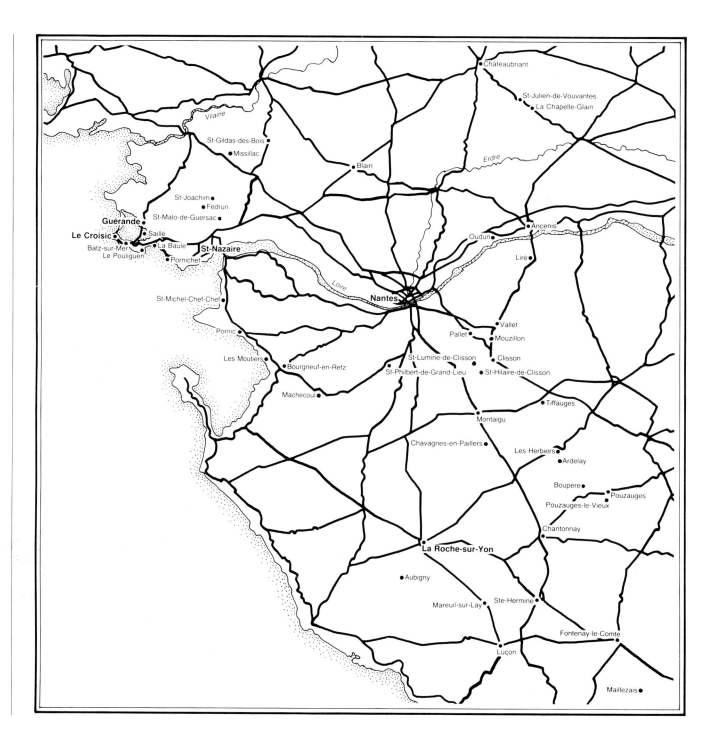

1
The Atlantic Coast

Nantes − Saint-Gildas-des-Bois − Batz-sur-Mer −
Guérande − Saint-Philbert-de-Grand-Lieu −
Châteaubriant − Ancenis − Tiffauges −
La Roche-sur-Yon

The interior of Nantes Cathedral is beautifully light and white. I arrived there at ten o'clock one Sunday morning just as Mass was beginning. Behind the nave altar a choir was singing a French hymn, to the tune of 'Abide with me'. In that early light the modern, not particularly inspired stained-glass windows at the east end seemed inoffensive and the light green windows at the sides did not intrude, allowing the vigorous tracery to make its own effect.

Nantes Cathedral was begun in 1434 and not finished for another 459 years. (The outside was never totally finished, though its three great portals and west facade are impressive enough.) Twice in our own times the building has suffered grievous damage, by bombing in 1944, when the sacristy and the chapels of the apse on the south side were completely destroyed, and by fire in 1972. In spite of these vicissitudes, the interior of this cathedral, now completely restored, has contrived to remain a perfectly harmonious gothic masterpiece.

Of course at Mass one is expected to join in the worship or at least to sit quietly. As ever in Nantes Cathedral I did not, for this gothic house of prayer houses in the south transept a superb renaissance tomb that is both touching and architecturally stunning. (I had also been told that owing to restoration work it would soon be hidden from the public gaze for some time.) This tomb is the last resting place of François II, Duke of Brittany, and his second wife, Marguerite de Foix. Michel Colombe − the greatest of all Breton sculptors − created it at the beginning of the sixteenth century. François and Marguerite lie hoping for eternal life, sculpted on a black slab of marble, guarded by angels, apostles, saints, and effigies representing justice, moderation, prudence and strength. (My favourite of these effigies is justice, if only for her beautifully braided hair and utterly blank expression.)

The man who lies here was of some importance in the history of this region. When King Charles VIII of France wanted to annex Brittany to his realms, François II put up a fierce resistance. The Breton troops were no match for the French army and were defeated in 1488, the year François died, at the battle of Saint-Aubin-du-Cornier. François gave the hand of his daughter Anne in marriage to Charles, and Brittany became French. The union was ratified in the château − south of the cathedral − which today dominates both Nantes and the place de-la-Duchesse-Anne.

This château is Nantes' second masterpiece: an extraordinary mixture of gothic and renaissance

architecture, two massive towers guarding its entrance. Many Loire châteaux today display this pleasing mixture of styles. That of Nantes was the first of its kind. The fortress and moat were constructed in the thirteenth century. Two centuries later François rebuilt it, and a century after his death it was again splendidly embellished. Here on 13 April 1598 King Henri IV signed the famous Edict of Nantes, giving a large measure of toleration to French protestants until Louis XIV revoked it in 1685.

For the Loire valley was a bastion of protestantism (though always catholics were in the majority). The word Huguenot derives from a tower at Tours, a favourite meeting-place for French protestants, named after King Hugon. John Calvin himself pursued his legal studies at Orléans. At Saumur the Governor Duplessis-Mornay founded a protestant academy, and protestants there seemed to be gaining the upper hand over catholicism for a time. At Blois the protestants murdered their arch-enemy Henri of Guise, head of the Catholic League. At Amboise they planned to kidnap the youthful king François II, but were discovered and subject to carnage themselves. The stench of rotting corpses was so great that the court temporarily quitted Amboise.

A boy of seven, Théodore Agrippa d'Aubigné, watched the slaughter of his protestant friends at Amboise and vowed to avenge them. He became not only a great Huguenot soldier but also wrote gifted poetry, into which he poured some of his hatred of what he had seen. He described naked, tortured bodies of men and women, the pitiful crying of their children, hanging upside-down from their feet, and the moans of other human beings hanging from their fingers or

The fancifully ornate well in the courtyard of the château at Nantes. Note the playful gothic dormer windows on the stern facade of the wing.

bound to wood and placed on the fire. To him the whole quarrel was foreshadowed in the Old Testament tale of the murder of Abel by his brother Cain. (Naturally, for Agrippa d'Aubigné, Abel was the innocent protestant, Cain the wrathful catholic):

'With a pure conscience Abel offered
Sacrifices to God. Cain also offered:
The one with a gentle spirit, the other hard-hearted.
One was acceptable to God, the other rejected.
Cain ground his teeth, and turned pale, appalling,
And massacred his brother, and of that sweet lamb
Made a sacrifice to his own wrathful bitterness.'

Hell, d'Aubigné concluded, could not hold enough dead to punish such a crime.

Nantes itself, before becoming the principal city of French religious toleration, received a notable protestant as prisoner. In 1547 the Castle of St Andrews in Scotland surrendered to the French. The Scottish Reformer John Knox was taken prisoner, brought to Nantes and served two years in the galleys.

John Knox's punishment incidentally indicates the source of the prosperity and strategic importance of Nantes. The city was the greatest seaport of Brittany. For this reason it was long coveted by the medieval counts of Anjou. Henry II of England took it without a struggle in 1156, and his brother Geoffrey became Count of Anjou. In subsequent centuries Nantes prospered as the chief port of western France, trading with the Indies and America, her merchants profiting from the slave trade and making vast fortunes from importing ebony. Richelieu in the early seventeenth century described Nantes as 'better able than any other city in the whole province to establish great trading links, transporting countless commodities along the River Loire to the great benefit of our realm'. In the next century 1300 vessels belonging to this city sailed the high seas, and the merchant-princes of Nantes built their noble residences on either side of the river. Only after the French Revolution, when the

23

British blockaded France and the slave trade was abolished, did their fortunes start to decline. The lower part of the Loire began to silt up, and great ships could no longer navigate as far as the city. Saint-Nazaire was developed as an alternative port. The picturesque Nantes-Brest canal proved an increasingly vital link with the sea.

Yet, partly as a result of this decline, Nantes remains a virtually unspoilt city, the seventh largest in France, rich in art and monuments. Savage air-raids in World War II left Nantes with 2000 dead, 3000 wounded, 1200 buildings destroyed, another 10,000 damaged and nearly 11,000 houses uninhabitable. The city has splendidly restored itself, its surviving old houses (such as those that overhang rue Bossuet), its carved porches and eighteenth-century wrought-iron balconies, its rugged porte Saint-Pierre (the old gateway into the city) still dominating. Today Nantes divides into two: an old part, dating from the Middle Ages to the eighteenth century (now a protected historical monument), and the modern, still charming city.

Walk west from the cathedral along rue Général-Leclerc and you reach the seventeenth-century town hall of Nantes (its splendid doorway dates from 1814). French cities have a penchant for sporting marvellous town halls, none finer than those of the Loire valley. This one is a complex of no fewer than three earlier 'hôtels': the hôtel de Derval (1605), the hôtel de Rosmadec (1666) and the late seventeenth-century hôtel Monti de Rézé.

Now go due south along rue Saint-Léonard, turn right along the delightfully named rue des Trois-Croissants, and find across the wide cours des Cinquante-Ôtages (so named after fifty hostages murdered by the Nazis in 1941) the nineteenth-century gothic church of Saint-Nicolas. To me this church exactly reverses the aesthetic pleasure of the cathedral. Though lovely inside, what impresses most of all is its magnificent exterior, especially its superb spire.

Southwest of the church of Saint-Nicolas lies place Royale, boasting an exquisite fountain with bacchic revellers and elegant ladies, some reclining, some stern and upright, all dripping wet. Now climb elegant rue Crébillon – the favourite street in Nantes for window-shoppers – as far as place Graslin. Here stands the Théâtre Graslin, completed, as an inscription proudly proclaims, in 1788 in the thirteenth year of the reign of Louis XVI. (One cannot avoid reflecting that he had only four more years to live before being guillotined.) The streets leading off this square are fittingly named after great French dramatists: rue Racine, rue Corneille and – to the right of the theatre – rue Molière which leads to 'Rue Scribe, auteur dramatique 1791–1861', whoever he was. Do not miss the pretty statue of three dancers by Charles Correia behind the theatre, placed here in 1982. Looking out at them from the theatre wall, on a *trompe l'oeil* balcony in front of a *trompe l'oeil* window, stand three figures: a muse, a young lady, and a little lad standing on a pile of books to look over the balcony; very jolly.

Half-way up rue Crébillon, on the left, is the passage Pommeraye, a marvellously romantic, mid nineteenth-century glass-roofed shopping arcade. The land is falling here, and the architect brilliantly utilized this natural feature of Nantes to create three levels of arcades. In this sumptuous gallery of stucco, statues and staircases you can buy books, boxing gloves, golf clubs, pullovers, bric-à-brac, paintings, make-up, false noses, prints and furs.

The city has of course much more to offer the tourist. Seeking the glories of medieval France one can easily neglect a nineteenth-century treasure-house at Nantes: the museum of fine arts in rue Clemenceau, to the east of the cathedral. This imposing example of civic

The noted, slightly comical seventeenth-century belfry of the church of Sainte-Croix, Nantes.

pride, erected in 1893, houses treasures which range from Italian primitives (such as Sano di Pietro's gentle painting of St Francis of Assisi receiving the stigmata) to magnificent, scarcely-known pictures by famous Italian mannerists. The nineteenth-century masters represented here include Ingres, Delacroix and Courbet. Undoubtedly the best-loved painting in this museum is that of a yawning old hurdy-gurdy player by Georges de la Tour. I must confess that I have often felt like him, tramping round museums of fine arts, and not only in Nantes.

If you would like to visit another outstanding museum, try the Musée Dobrée (north of rue Voltaire) in a building designed by Viollet-le-Duc a year after the museum of fine arts was built. It contains an astonishingly rich selection of enamels, old armour, pewter, Roman glass, old views of the city of Nantes and the like, all bequeathed by an indefatigable collector named Thomas Dobrée. My own taste prefers Viollet-le-Duc's lovely museum to most of its contents.

Nantes in truth presents me with more museums than I can easily digest. The rest include a museum of Breton popular art in the ducal château; the museum of naval history nearby; and *La Psallette*, a lovely fifteenth-century building to the south of the cathedral square, housing a fine collection of religious art.

Nantes is the chief city of the *département* of Loire-Atlantique, created in 1790, including part of the southern section of the old duchy of Brittany. (Until 1957 it was known by the far less pleasing name of Loire-Inférieure.) Dolmens, ancient burial grounds, menhirs and the like indicate that the whole eastern part of Loire-Atlantique was extensively occupied in prehistoric times. The city itself was built where the River Erdre meets the Loire. The Loire here momentarily divides, forming one arm called 'la Madeleine' and another, the 'bras de Pirmil'. As a result Nantes incorporates its own mini-island, the Île de la Prairie-au-Duc, now devoted to shipping and shipyards. The great river flows through the *département*, from Ancenis in the east to Saint-Nazaire on the Atlantic coast, with Nantes dominating the centre of the whole region.

Nearly 7000 square kilometres in all, Loire-Atlantique is a varied land: the many different soils were brought here by rivers long ago. Around Redon rich pastureland nourishes milk cows. Beef cattle graze around Châteaubriant and Ancenis. Market-gardens abound in the southern lands around Machecoul and to the west by Guérande. The *département* boasts a fantastic natural park – la Brière – renowned wines, and in La Baule what the French rightly describe as the finest beach in Europe. Here the magnolia was first cultivated in Europe. An eighteenth-century French sailor, Barin de La Galissonnière, brought plants from the banks of the Mississippi and raised them in his arboretum, on an estate whose crumbled walls you can still see by the side of the N149 just as you approach Pallet from Nantes. In Nantes itself the splendid magnolias and camellias of the Jardin des Plantes (a short walk east from the cathedral square along rue Clemenceau) are witness to the enterprising Galissonnière, to the city's colonial past, and to the fecundity that results from the soil and climate of this part of the Loire valley.

No one visiting Loire-Atlantique should neglect its cuisine. Naturally the rivers offer succulent white pike, which is here served poached in white butter sauce (*brochet beurre blanc*). Normally I do not like duck, but *canard nantais* is to my palate somehow different. The people of Brittany also cherish their own traditional foods, usually cooked very gently over a low flame. Ask for *poulet en barbouille* if you think you

One of the enchanting thatched cottages that have stood in the Brière natural park for centuries. This one is between Missillac and Saint-Lyphard.

will relish a chicken whose sauce has been enriched with its own blood, its own chopped liver, cream and the yolk of an egg.

As for wines, the vineyards of Loire-Atlantique cover 12,500 hectares. These produce each year 400,000 hectolitres of Muscadet and 100,000 hectolitres of Gros Plant, as well as the Gamay grown in the vineyards on the slopes around Ancenis. The best-known of these wines, Muscadet, comes basically in three sorts: straightforward *appellation contrôlée* Muscadet, grown in a wide area around Nantes and south of the river almost to its estuary; the *appellation* known as 'Coteaux-de-la-Loire', which is nearly all grown north of the river around Ancenis; and – the most famous – 'appellation Sèvre et Maine contrôlée', grown between the two little rivers Sèvre and Maine. These fruity wines perfectly complement the fish cooked so superbly in this whole region, and trout cooked in Muscadet (*truite au Muscadet*) is a tangy delight.

Oddly enough, the excellence of the wines of this part of the Loire valley partly derives from those of Burgundy. The Romans cultivated vines on either side of the river, and medieval monks developed their own traditions of viticulture here. Then, at the beginning of the eighteenth century, frost destroyed all the vines of the Loire. The vignerons turned to a white Burgundy grape called the 'Melon de Bourgogne', discovered that it was perfectly at home on their slopes and have never looked back. Today you can visit in the ducal château at Nantes the cellar (with an ancient wooden wine-press and other vintners' knick-knacks) that now belongs to the Company of 'Bretvins', a group dedicated to praising 'at all times and in all places' the wines of the region – in my view not a difficult task.

Corn ripening by green forests in the Loire valley.

It is time to leave Nantes and explore the rest of Loire-Atlantique. The *département* is to my mind at its most romantic in autumn, its undulating countryside a mixture of chestnuts and evergreens, and with solitary men on stools, fishing in the Nantes-Brest Canal.

Drive northwest for several kilometres along the N165 to Missillac and turn right for another 10 kilometres as far as the village of Saint-Gildas-des-Bois. Here in 1026 Benedictine monks founded a monastery (dedicated to the sixth-century St Gildas) that is still inhabited, though today by nuns, not monks. The revolutionaries suppressed the house in 1790. Nuns have returned here to run a hospital for cripples. You can wander without hindrance through its woods with their many grottoes and welcome seats, past the domestic architecture, the nuns' garden where their washing hangs out to dry, the seventeenth-century wing and the colonnaded hospital. Here I suffered an embarrassing religious experience one Saturday morning. Entering the modernistic twelve-sided chapel I found myself unexpectedly behind the altar, in between a priest and deacon celebrating Mass for the nuns and the patients (many of them in wheelchairs and on stretchers). Graciously welcoming the intruder, the sisters indicated that I ought to sit at the back.

It is probably less perilous to explore the parish church outside the walls of the convent. In 1711 its rood-screen was built to separate the pious monks from the other rustic worshippers. The north transept houses a statue of a gentle Virgin Mary, sculpted in stone in the fourteenth century. In the south transept stands a statue of St Sebastian which miraculously turned aside the plague that was threatening Saint-Gildas-des-Bois in 1595.

Drive back to Missillac, which seems to have so little to commend itself that you might easily miss the beautiful fifteenth-century château just to the south. Splendidly restored (for the revolutionaries burnt it down), Château de la Bretesche is in two parts, at the

Left The fifteenth-century Château de la Bretesche (beautifully restored in the nineteenth century), seen across its lake south of Missillac. Notice the hexagonal towers and the massive round one, the oldest of all.

Above A quiet country path and open gates belie the once savage history of the Loire valley.

31

far side of an artificial blue, green and white lake, its steep roofs, little turrets, dormer windows, crenellations and chimneys all nestling amongst the woods. (One part of the château has stone chimneys, the other brick.)

Close by are welcome picnic sites and a golf course. And soon it is time to abandon your car to range at least part of the 7000 hectares of peat bog which constitute the remarkable natural park of the Brière. Drive south by way of thatched cottages, some of them in splendid condition, some tumbledown, as far as the hamlet of Saint-Joachim, and turn right to the village of Fédrun, where you can take a punt through the streams and dikes of this region of wildfowlers and fishermen. At nearby Saint-Malo-de-Guersac is a museum and animal park (open only in summer – to my annoyance, since, as I have confessed, I infinitely prefer the Loire-Atlantique in autumn). Even in summer you need to wear wellington boots for it is muddy in the animal park.

Now drive southeast towards Saint-Nazaire, finding the road to La Baule in order to reach the Atlantic coast. This is a region of beautiful shrubs and flowers for those who can spot them: the pink-and-white striped convolvulus which pushes up through the pebbles of the beach; the pink sea *armérie*; the yellow flowers of the horned pavot, which you find by turning aside its thick green leaves; the rudely-named 'rubbery carrot', with its impressive red flower; the large daisies that are known here as *maritime matricaires*; the purple-pink arborescent *lavatère*, whose leaves are even more off-putting than those of the horned pavot; the thick purple flowers of the *giroflées* which populate the sand-dunes; the delicate yellow wild pimpernel rose; the red coastal plant which is called hare's tail; the tough sea-grape with its yellow blooms; and the bizarre orange red fingers of the European salicorne.

La Baule is a thriving seaside resort – not surprisingly in view of its astonishingly clean, sandy and welcoming bay. Reading its history I find it amazing that no one spotted its potential as a holiday resort until the early twentieth century. The pine woods that so enhance the coast were originally planted not to entrance tourists but to anchor the shifting sands. The modern boulevard is wide and tree-lined (and partly pedestrianized). Every holiday facility is here: tennis, golf, a casino, restaurants, bars and fine hotels. This tourists' Sahara of a beach extends south as far as the contiguous seaside resort of Pornichet. A century ago Pornichet was no more than a fishing hamlet. Local fishermen still sail out to bring back catches of sweet sardines. But today the two arms of its sheltered harbour embrace many more pleasure boats than fishing smacks.

Close by is the seaside resort of Le Pouliguen. If ever seaside holidays cease to be part of the self-indulgence of Western civilization, Le Pouliguen will remain beautiful. It shares the same fantastic sandy bay as La Baule. Gnarled rock formations add a slightly frightening grandeur to the coastline (reminding one of what an ocean can carve out of the mainland). Today Le Pouliguen is partly tamed by its yachts, its tennis and golf clubs, all the appurtenances of summer holidays. Yet the ocean is still slightly menacing. All along the coast, by the sweetly named Bay of St Mary (*Baie de la Bonne Vierge*), the Cave of the Chapel (*Grotte de la Chapelle*), and Samson's peak (*Rocher de Samson*) are notices warning *prudence*.

On then, carefully, *avec prudence*, 3 kilometres to Batz-sur-Mer. Here they board up their windows in winter against the Atlantic gales that tear up trees in the natural park of Brière. Batz-sur-Mer has been braving these storms since it was founded by Benedictine monks in the year 945. In the place du Murier stands the ruins of its romantic church, Saint-Guénole-de-Batz, with its late seventeenth-century bell-tower rising 60 metres. The south porch of the church of Notre Dame de Batz shelters a wooden Madonna and Child, her hair brushed back as she blesses us. The locals tell you that the nave of Notre

Dame de Batz inclines to one side as does the suffering head of the Christ hanging on the crucifix of its high altar.

This is still quintessential Brittany, and here are the twisting streets of an old Breton village. The *boulangerie-pâtisserie* sells those lovely butter biscuits known as *Galettes de Bretonnes*; and round the corner leather clogs with wooden soles festoon the front of the *Maison du Sabot*. Inside you can buy wooden shoes. And on weekdays the clog-maker of Batz-sur-Mer still carves clogs out of logs of wood in the old-fashioned way, under an umbrella in the main square of the town.

Three kilometres northwest along the coast from Batz-sur-Mer you reach Le Croisic. Yachts ride the Atlantic. Other yachts and motor-boats are tied up at the little picturesque harbour. Once on the end of the peninsula, outside Le Croisic itself, the crooked rocks left by the savage, attacking sea become more menacing, beautiful and dangerous, sometimes virtually tumbling into the waters. On our right are windswept pines. Warning flags mark submerged rocks.

It is easy to picture the Normans, repeatedly returning to pillage Le Croisic. The little harbour began to prosper only in the fifteenth century. The citizens felt secure enough to build two chapels in the next century, one (Saint-Crucifix) in a splendid flamboyant style. Today they devote themselves to fishing, glass-making and caring for tourists. To my mind too many visitors spoil this farouche coast. I can remember happily picnicking on the shore just outside the port one October, the sun still shining, no one else around at noon, the local *charcuterie* having provided meats, a glass of Muscadet waiting for me on a rock. In the distance a few people were fishing. Then two men arrived with jars and fishing-nets to prospect in the pools left by the retreating tide. As they passed they called out 'Bon Appétit', and I asked what they were after. 'Crevettes' was the answer, big ones an excellent dish, the smaller ones preferable to serve as bait for bigger fish. Silence returned. But as I threw away my bits of bread, seagulls came to eat them. From behind a rock appeared a magnificent, but limping, brown-and-white bird, a kind of cormorant – though I could not properly identify it. Every time I threw it its own piece of bread, the seagulls swooped and stole the morsel. I tried to pick up the injured bird, but the poor lame creature limped away. It tried to bury itself behind a rock, and I drove away to Guérande, leaving the forlorn creature behind.

From Le Croisic drive back to La Baule and turn north towards the central town of this peninsula (or *presque'île*, as the French call it): Guérande. The route passes a lovely old white windmill before reaching the powerfully fortified village of Saillé, with its long low salt pans where men still gather in the salt with long rakes. The salt-bearing water readily evaporates in shallow basins scooped out in the earth. Notre-Dame-du-Murier, the church at Batz, is quaintly dedicated to Our Lady of Sea-Salt. If the history of salt fascinates you, call in at the house of the Paludier (salt-gatherer) next to the church at Saillé. When the salt is first gathered here, it is frequently a charming pink, the effect of micro-organisms. These soon die, allowing the salt then to turn a fine grey in colour. Buy a little bagful from a paludier and then drive on to Guérande.

Guérande is protected by ancient walls that are almost intact, and by fortified fifteenth-century gates – the salvation of the town when Saracens, Normans and Spaniards successively invaded and pillaged this part of Brittany. Porte Saint-Michel, the earliest of the four gates, has two massive towers with conical hats resolutely defending the town to the west. Guérande existed as long ago as neolithic times, and was converted to Christianity in the third century by St Clair, the first Bishop of Nantes. For centuries since those turbulent invasions of the Middle Ages, the town seems to have quietly slept and – even when invaded by tourists – it preserves a magical calm.

Below West of Le Croisic the Atlantic coast is defended by slightly menacing twisted granite rocks, moulded into shape over centuries by the ocean.

Right Fishing boats moored beside a propellor and an old anchor in the sheltered harbour of Le Croisic.

Honoré de Balzac was referring to Guérande in his *Beatrix* when he described a town 'still standing but not yet fully alive, with no apparent *raison d'être* save that no one had yet demolished her. The effect on one's soul is as if you had just taken a tranquillizer.'

Inside the town walls, Guérande with its higgeldy-piggeldy streets is a gem. At the west end of the church of Saint-Aubin, built between the eleventh and the fourteenth centuries, is an open-air pulpit. Inside, carved at the top of the pillars, you can find St Lawrence being grilled on his grid-iron, St Simon being sawn in two and St Stephen being stoned, as well as jugglers, the Holy Grail, and the rich miser being chastised for not giving to poor Lazarus. The church houses an ancient sarcophagus dating from the second half of the sixth century. Spare time for its sixteenth-century stained glass, depicting (north of the high altar) scenes from the life of St Peter: about to walk on the water, being crucified upside-down, and so on. On the other side of the high altar is a tiny chapel with an ancient font. And the woodwork of the pulpit is superb, even if the carved dove representing the Holy Spirit does look more like a seagull.

Within sight of the church of Saint-Aubin, on the way to the fifteenth-century porte Bizienne, is the perfectly unified fourteenth-century chapel of Notre-Dame-de-la-Blanche.

From Guérande an easy road runs 17 kilometres southeast to Saint-Nazaire. During World War II parts of this important port were continually being blown up by the allied forces. One particularly audacious raid was carried out on 28 May 1942 by eighteen British commandos who penetrated the German defences to lay five tonnes of explosives. The town was almost completely destroyed in 1945. As a result, Saint-Nazaire today is a new, friendly, functional, architecturally boring town, the creation of its borough architect M. Le Maresquier.

It possesses a superb toll-bridge over the estuary of the Loire, a toll well worth paying, not only to save a long detour but also because there is a marvellous view of sea and shipping from the bridge. Drive on speedily south from here to see two insufficiently celebrated treasures of Brittany: the village of Les Moutiers and, at Saint-Philbert-de-Grand-Lieu to southeast, the oldest church in France.

This, though an easy drive, is quite a long way. The road passes through the quaintly named village of Saint-Michel-Chef-Chef, with its fishermen's cottages and the ruined tower of its medieval château. The church at Saint-Michel-Chef-Chef is modern, though built in the renaissance style. Another diversion would be to call at the seaside town of Pornic. As well as offering more of the hospitable Sahara that constitutes this coastline, Pornic is where 200 Vendéens lie buried, their graves in the cemetery dominated by a seventeenth-century cross, known as the Cross of the Huguenots.

Be ready for the sign pointing right to Les Moutiers, with its medieval priory church and its shady village square. Outside the church is one of those bizarre 'lanterns of the dead' that are sparsely dotted around France and some parts of Germany. Inside the lantern is a circular stone staircase which people would climb to set light to the candle at the top when a coffin was brought here. Did they, I wonder, put the coffin on the slab in front of the lantern, while the mourners protected themselves from the grim reaper by dipping into the holy water stoup at the side, hoping also for a blessing from the Madonna and Child whose statue adorns this slender tower?

Your eyes adjust to the light inside the church at Les Moutiers until you catch a glimpse of the wide, barrel-vaulted roof. The seventeenth-century high altar is

---

The walls and massive fifteenth-century Porte Saint-Michel at Guérande. Note the pulleys in between the towers, once used for lowering and lifting a drawbridge.

An ancient cannon points out to sea at the strategic Pointe de Saint-Gildas (west of Pornic), a reminder of times when this part of the Loire valley was continually ravaged by marauders.

amazingly rich, once you have made it out in the gloom, decorated with cherubs and saints, and depicting in the centre (in an early nineteenth-century painting) Jesus giving the keys of the kingdom of heaven to St Peter. The parish priest claims that the picture of the Madonna (with her child in swaddling clothes already standing upright on her knee) is Florentine. It was torn in two by impious hands at the time of the Revolution, and one of the present priest's recent predecessors (the Abbé Coëllier) had it restored.

Drive back to the main road and go on through Bourgneuf-en-Retz to Machecoul. No longer is the ambience that of Brittany, though technically speaking we are still in that region. This is the Pays de Retz, the countryside above all of the notorious child-murderer Gilles de Retz, Marshal of France, the legendary Bluebeard and friend of Joan of Arc, who for his sins was hanged and burned at Nantes in 1440.

Machecoul is the capital of this historically nefarious land. King Henri III elevated the barony of Retz to a dukedom in 1581 because of the services the baron had rendered France. But all that remains of the duke's fortress here is a ruin. To find it you must drive all the way through this sleepy town, past its quiet market hall. If it is difficult to believe that the debaucher Gilles de Retz could once have lived in this charming town, it is scarcely credible that in 1793 the terrifying, vicious counter-revolutionary revolt of the Vendée also began here.

Sixteen kilometres east of Machecoul lies Saint-Philbert-de-Grand-Lieu. The name of this village derives from the Abbé Filibert who founded a monastery here in the year 676. The oldest surviving church in France is certainly not the massive Saint-Remi in the centre of Saint-Philbert-de-Grand-Lieu. Saint-Remi was built between 1862 and 1869. A notice inside courteously tells you that this is not the church you are looking for.

From the other end of the place de l'Église (on the north side of Saint-Remi), rue de la Poste leads to the ninth-century Carolingian abbey church. Started on the eve of Charlemagne's death and finished in 819, it stands – as every monastery had to – on the banks of a river. Filibert himself lies in a sarcophagus in the crypt, his body brought here in 839 in a five-day journey on the backs of monks fleeing the savage Normans. Twenty-two years later Norman marauders forced the hapless monks to take their precious corpse

The seaside resort of Pornic offers not only a superb beach but also lovely old houses, a fourteenth-century château (to the right of the picture) and a church with a splendid seventeenth-century bell-tower.

to Tournus, but bits of the holy relic were brought back here again. The choir had been rebuilt in honour of Filibert's corpse in 836. The Normans burned down the nave in 847, so that too had to be rebuilt. Everything today is being meticulously restored.

The ancient church of Saint-Philbert-de-Grand-Lieu is cool and simple, its romanesque arches humbly decorated with slender bricks. The west facade is virtually blank: a pointed arch for the doorway, three round windows high up, two buttresses stopping the whole facade from falling down. On the south side another two powerful buttresses are reflected in still water. The north wall, buttressed equally powerfully, adjoins lawns and seats, where I have eaten picnic lunches. The interior is extraordinary. The pillars suddenly bulge, as if the builders did not trust their judgment, as if they feared the whole edifice might suddenly tumble down unless they took special precautions to keep it up.

From Saint-Philbert-de-Grand-Lieu back to Nantes is no more than 25 kilometres along good roads. But if you really want to explore Loire-Atlantique properly you must now be prepared for a round trip of 80 kilometres, north from Nantes to Blain and Château-briant and back to Ancenis further up the River Loire. To reach Blain you drive north from Nantes past the hippodrome, in the direction of Rennes (N137). This route takes you past the open-air sports centre of Nantes, and if the sun is shining you could drive off the main road here and make a picnic on the benches under the trees or even join the activities of the endless groups of joggers and sports fanatics. Thirteen

The château and gardens at Blain. The twin towers were built in the fourteenth century, contrasting with the jolly renaissance wing with its stone mullions and dormers and its gothicized chimneys.

kilometres out of Nantes, turn left along the D16 and then right along the D37 to join the D164 to Blain.

I find the village of Blain unprepossessing and its church quite hideous. The delights lie just outside the village. Follow the signs leading towards the château and the Nantes-Brest canal. Drive through an unsafe-looking arch (with many bits knocked off its lower stones by careless carters) to the fierce château, the earliest part rebuilt in the thirteenth century (with some later additions, such as the massive Tour de Connétable, which dates from 1380).

Its walls look out over what was once a moat. Its gargoyles are half-animal, half-human, with the devil as a goat to represent the more regrettable aspects of our natures. A blend of every style and material (gothic, renaissance, brick, sandy mortar and stone), this lovely mixture of a château happens today to be a day-school for architecturally fortunate children (as the little row of outdoor toilets and the children's sports field indicate).

The road back to the village of Blain passes over the canal, and if you immediately turn right here you come upon a delightful sheltered harbour, with a café, a restaurant and a hotel.

For half an hour you now drive through Muscadet country – with ample opportunity for tasting fine wines – along the N171 to Châteaubriant. En route I mostly like to sample the fruity, slightly dry 'Gros Plant du Pays Nantais', especially that modestly dubbed only 'VDQS' (i.e., much better than ordinary table wine but not so good as *appellation contrôlée*), which is very refreshing and does not make me want to go to sleep in the afternoon.

The citizens of Châteaubriant will tell you that their home is basically Celtic. To me it seems essentially feudal, enclosed by fourteenth-century walls, draw-bridges and sternly fortified gates. Perhaps its château contradicts my judgment, for half of it is renaissance – rough-hewn stones deliberately contrasted with slate and finely-cut mullions. Even so, the ancient keep

41

Renaissance loggia and pavilion at Châteaubriant. In this town in 1487 King Charles VIII and the dukes of Brittany signed a historic agreement which led eventually to the union of Brittany with France.

dominates all these later fripperies. Especially to the north, on the lakeside, this fortress presents the dourly formidable aspect of the Middle Ages. The old wash-houses under its ramparts transport one's imagination back through centuries of toiling women.

Inside the walls of Châteaubriant, as well as finding the splendid church of Saint-Jean-de-Béré, look for the ancient market hall, where rue Aristide Briant running north–south meets the Grand'rue running east–west. It has been transformed into a pretty modern art gallery. In the half-timbered house on the corner of rue de Couëré once lived Sophie Trebuchet. On 15 November 1797 she met Captain Léopold Sigisbert. She married him in Paris and in 1802 bore their son, Victor Hugo.

The way back to Ancenis from Châteaubriant takes you along the D163 by way of Saint-Julien-de-Vouvantes. At Châteaubriant I could find little good to say about the twentieth-century church of Saint-Nicolas. At Saint-Julien-de-Vouvantes, by contrast, is a quite impressive modern church, covering a fourteenth-century crypt and housing some lovely old stone statues: a fourteenth-century Virgin Mary with St Anne; a fifteenth-century St Benedict; a seventeenth-century St René; and two eighteenth-century angels carved in wood. The road runs between the church and a 400-year-old house with 400-year-old turrets. Soon we reach the fifteenth-century battlemented château of La Motte-Glain and turn right (at the village of La Chapelle-Glain) to take first the D878 and then the D923 south to Ancenis. As you cross over the motorway outside Ancenis, to your left appears what seems at first sight to be an ancient ruined viaduct; it is in truth a disused army shooting range.

Ancenis bears the scars of an old strategic frontier town, situated on the southern border of Brittany. Its walls are little more than broken-down defences. At the end of the tenth century the seigneurs of Nantes built its château as a bastion against the territorial ambitions of the rival counts of Anjou. The English took it during the Hundred Years War, and King Louis VII of France took it back again. In the fifteenth century it three times withstood sieges by the expanding kingdom of the French, and when he finally took it Charles VIII tore it down. Rebuilt in the sixteenth century, the château was where Duke François II of Brittany finally capitulated to Louis XI of France.

Henri IV was the next king to besiege the château of Ancenis, in the early sixteenth century. Louis XIII dismantled most of it in the early seventeenth century, leaving the town virtually defenceless. A century and a half later Ancenis was pillaged by the counter-revolutionary Vendéens. It therefore comes as something of a surprise to find anything at all of its walls and château. In fact you can still see the great gate of the fifteenth-century building, with its massive machicolated towers, and the renaissance part that the Angevin architect Jean de l'Espine designed in 1535, as well as the elegant seventeenth-century pavilions.

The parish church at Ancenis displays a similar pleasing mix of styles: a medieval apse and a partly renaissance nave. Here too, in a prosperous modern town, have survived a good number of charming medieval houses, especially around the market square and along rue des Tonneliers, the lower Grand'rue and rue du Château. Follow the picturesque medieval pattern of winding, twisting streets. On the slopes outside Ancenis modern industry has not hampered the cultivation of the crisp white wine known as 'les côteaux d'Ancenis-Gamay' which (like 'Gros Plant du Pays Nantais') was granted the accolade *vin délimitée de qualité supérieure* in 1954.

The River Loire at Ancenis – ancient frontier town that still shows the scars of its turbulent past.

If you are driving back towards Nantes from Ancenis, after ten minutes you come across another reminder of the dangers that faced any frontier town or village in the Middle Ages: the impressive octagonal watch-tower of Oudon, 32 metres high, battlemented, aggressive. The château to which this keep belonged changed hands again and again in the turbulent Middle Ages. It was taken in 1174 by King Henry II of England. John Lackland captured it in 1214. Louis IX retook it for the French in 1230. In 1341 Charles de Blois besieged it and overcame its defenders. Alan de Malestroit rebuilt the keep, as it substantially still stands, in 1390. In July and August you can climb the tower and perceive what are today merely superb panoramas of the surrounding countryside, but what were then vistas-incessantly and anxiously scanned for the first glimpse of advancing enemies.

I prefer not to drive west from Ancenis but south over the graceful suspension bridge that spans the river. A nineteenth-century statue of the sixteenth-century poet Joachim du Bellay stands facing this bridge, for he was born in 1522 at Liré south of the river. He published a defence of the French vernacular tongue in 1549, which became the manifesto of a group of poets headed by Ronsard and later known as *la Pléiade*. His own love-poetry was inspired by the sonnets of Petrarch, and dedicated to a Mademoiselle de la Viole. Du Bellay disguised this lady's identity by dubbing her *l'Olive*, a scarcely concealed anagram of her real name.

Joachim du Bellay died young, aged only thirty-seven, though he had made a name for himself both in Paris and in Rome (where he was secretary to his uncle Cardinal Jean du Bellay). In Rome he wrote exquisite verses nostalgically longing for the place of his birth:

Alas, when shall I see again smoke rising
From the chimneys of my tiny village; when shall I see again
The meadow of my humble house?

Far more than the Latin Tiber my Gallic Loire
    delights me;
Far more my little Liré than this mount Palatine;
And far more Angevin sweetness than the maritime
    air of Rome.

He remembered winnowing the corn in the wind of the
Loire valley:

> You gentle breath
> Fanning that plain
> Fanning my stay there,
> Even though I toiled away
> At winnowing my corn
> In the heat of the day.

He remembered the flowers of his native land: violets,
lilies, roses and carnations. You can remember Joachim
du Bellay today in the museum set up in the Grand
Logis at his beloved Liré.

The rolling road south from Liré towards Clisson
traverses vineyards and shady woods. This is the *route
du vin* of Loire-Atlantique. The grapes grown here are
mostly Muscadet, Gros Plant and Gamay, with lots of
establishments inviting you to taste and buy their
wines. You pass through Vallet with its delightfully
named Château Noë-Bel-Air (mostly a nineteenth-
century reconstruction); and as you cross over the
rivulet at Mouzillon, look left at the tiny stone bridge
with four arches – one of them pointed – which the
Romans built.

The château at Clisson is a far more amiable ruin
than that at Ancenis. The portcullis is no more, but the
gateway is impressive, and it is still worth buying a
ticket to wander around its complex buildings. The
lords of Clisson built the oldest part of this château in
the thirteenth century. Two centuries later the
surrounding walls were built. The powerful keep is
approached by way of a primitive drawbridge, whose
chains still exist. Only one horseman at a time could get
in through these external defences.

Above **The medieval fortress at Clisson, built
between the thirteenth and fifteenth centuries,
dominates the confluence of the Rivers Sèvre
and Moine.**

Right **A more peaceful view of Clisson: the
nineteenth-century church of Our Lady, with its
Italianate bell-tower and its romanesque-style
apse, seen across the gentle River Sèvre.**

The interior was so hurriedly and shabbily built
that most of the buildings collapsed one Christmas Eve
in the seventeenth century. The well of the château
tells an even grimmer tale. During the Revolution, it is
said, the royalists had taken shelter here. Foolishly
they cooked in the great fireplace. The smoke betrayed
them. Their enemies forced their way into the château,
massacred the royalists and flung their bodies into this
well. They filled it with earth and planted a pine tree

on top. When the pine tree died many years later, the well was opened up again, and among the pathetic objects recovered was a child's shoe.

Clisson is on two rivers, the Sèvre and the little Moine. The waters and the town entranced Gustave Flaubert, forgetful of its savage past.

'On the side of a hill where two rivers meet,' he wrote, 'in a fresh countryside lit by the clear colours of roofs covered with tiles that could almost be Italian, close by a long cascade that turns a mill which you can scarcely see through the foliage, the château of Clisson displays its head crowned with huge trees. And outside the château everything is calm and gentle.'

Flaubert continued:

'The little houses laugh under a warm sky; you can hear the water rippling, flecks of moss floating on a current that drenches limp clumps of greenery.'

Tribes of hunters roamed the region of Clisson 10,000 years before the birth of Christ. The remains of modest dwellings have been found here, dating from 4000 BC. The Gauls flourished here, but by the time of the Revolution Clisson still housed no more than 2500 souls. On 18 May 1793 revolutionaries put to death the royalists of the town and burned down their houses. In September of that year, revolutionary troops commanded by Napoleon's General Kléber were routed by a force said to number 20,000 Vendéens. By the time the Revolution was over, Clisson was in ruins.

As you can see today, it rose again. Two architects, Lenot and Cacault, with a penchant for the Italian style, seized their opportunity. Clisson's old bridge is now flanked by elegant classical mills. The seventeenth-century market hall is redolent with must and charm. The citizens commissioned their architects to restore the parish church, still approached by old winding streets and narrow steps. They chose to enhance the romanesque style of the Loire valley with a splendid Italianate campanile.

Leaving Clisson en route for Les Herbiers to the southeast, you enter the Vendéen bocage, those woodlands whose inhabitants so ferociously took up arms 'for king and country' in 1793. A line of sombre granite hills runs northeast/southwest through the upper bocage. The territory is gentler now than it was 200 years ago, when Kléber's men could hardly force their way through the thickets to try to put down the Vendéens. Yet in spite of modern roads there are still areas of dense forest in the bocage, through which the sun scarcely penetrates.

Take the D755 to Les Herbiers, but make a detour left along the D753 to Tiffauges, to visit the superb ruined château of Gilles de Retz. This fascinating ruin lies just outside the village, dominating the confluence of the Rivers Sèvre and Crume. The name Tiffauges derives from the Tiffalian Scythians, a fearsome element in Caesar's legions, who established a camp here. The château was built by the Viscount of Thouars in the Middle Ages, and in the fifteenth century it became the favourite home of Gilles de Retz, husband of Catherine de Thouars.

Even before his time this château had earned a reputation for necromancy. Legend held that it was built by Melusine, the offspring of an unnatural liaison between King Elinas of Albania and a fairy. Each Saturday, condemned for her harshness towards her father, Melusine was fated to turn into a half-snake. She married Raymondin, nephew of the Count of Poitou, extracting from him a promise that he would never try to see her on a Saturday. Her magical powers made him rich, as she miraculously built him château after château. But her own strange blood revealed itself in their nine children, each of which was in some fashion curiously disfigured. And one day Raymondin forgot his matrimonial vow. On a Saturday evening he

Cattle graze by the river in this richly productive part of France.

entered the apartments of his fairy-wife. She was bathing, and to his horror, in spite of her long golden tresses, he saw that her naked body was that of a snake. Melusine fled through a window, leaving him for ever and as she went cursing her husband's châteaux. 'Tiffauges, Pouzauges . . ., each one shall crumble stone by stone as the years pass.' And so it has proved.

The career of Gilles de Retz was likewise marked by necromancy. Willing to solicit the help even of Satan himself in his attempt to find the philosopher's stone, surrounding himself with infamous magicians and alchemists, Gilles is said to have offered children as human sacrifices to the devil at Tiffauges. The impressive ruins of his château include a massive rectangular keep (the so-called Tour de Vidane), moats, a tower with vaulted chambers and a medieval fireplace, as well as the arcading of the romanesque chapel where Gilles de Retz sacrilegiously heard Mass.

From this fearful spot drive along the D9 to Les Herbiers. Just north of the village (after the road has joined the N160), you enjoy the panoramic views of the Mont des Alouettes, the hill of the larks, 243 metres above sea-level. Here stood seven windmills until four were burnt down in 1793, when the revolutionaries realized that they were being used by the Vendéens to signal republican troop movements to their allies.

When the monarchy was restored, 11,000 Vendéen soldiers stood on the Mont des Alouettes to be proudly presented to Louis XIV's daughter, the Duchess of Angoulême. The gothic chapel built out of granite in 1823 (but not completed till 1968) commemorates the occasion.

To see more parts of the Loire valley that blend history, literature and romantic charm you need to leave the easy roads at this point and drive south to Ardelay (though it is no distance), where you turn right as far as the lovely complex of buildings that constitutes the fine abbey of Notre-Dame-de-la-Grainetière. Built by Benedictines in the twelfth century, the white stone walls topped with orange tiles, the delicate colonnaded cloisters and the monastery cells are today occupied by brothers of the community of Our Lady of Hope. Here the Abbé Prévost wrote *Manon Lescaut*. This charming religious house seems gently to set itself against the viciousness of most of the rest of the history of the Vendéen bocage. But drive southeast towards Boupère and you will see how the citizens felt the need powerfully to fortify their thirteenth-century church of Saint-Pierre, to give themselves some chance of surviving the ever-threatening assaults of their enemies.

Pouzauges (reached by taking the D13 southeast to the D960, where you turn left) is another stronghold of

Pouzauges, known as 'the pearl of the bocage', displays its charms in a crumbling wall boasting seventeenth-century gateposts and wrought-iron gates.

Gilles de Retz. Its ruined château still has its keep, 18 square metres in plan and 27 metres high, surrounded by medieval ramparts with six round towers. Gilles de Retz's great hall still survives on the second storey of the keep. If you have time, drive on east to Pouzauges-le-Vieux, to look at its granite romanesque church, built in the eleventh and twelfth centuries in the form of a Latin cross, with a round fourteenth-century apse. In 1948 entrancing frescoes of the life of the Blessed Virgin Mary were uncovered on the north wall of the nave.

I would now drive southwest from the village of Pouzauges – whose straggling white houses have earned it the soubriquet 'pearl of the bocage' – through Chantonnay, where in 1793 the Vendéens defeated a force of 6000 supporters of the Revolution. Beyond Chantonnay about 20 kilometres to the west is La Roche-sur-Yon, a total surprise of a town. In 1794 La Roche-sur-Yon was completely razed by republican troops, leaving only its clock-tower, the ramparts of its château and the mill of La Garde on the road to Aubigny (D747). Napoleon Bonaparte decided that from here he could reassert his authority throughout the whole disaffected region. On 14 May 1804 he made La Roche-sur-Yon the capital of the Vendée. He rebuilt the town as a perfect example of the civil planning of the First Empire. A new church, a town hall, a grammar school, and law courts were built in the neo-classical style. The church of Saint-Louis is especially imposing: six Doric columns support a Greek pediment on its west facade, with two square towers rising from each corner. Inside, the nave is supported by eight fluted Corinthian columns. In the huge square fronting the church, a bronze statue of Napoleon himself (by Nieuwerkerque) rides towards the house of God.

La Roche-sur-Yon almost reaches the southernmost point of this part of the Loire valley. Drive further southeast through Mareuil-sur-Lay (which boasts a restored romanesque church) as far as Luçon. Cardinal Richelieu was bishop here in the early seventeenth century, and the episcopal palace is suitably grand, connected to the cathedral by eleventh-century cloisters. Richelieu also built himself another grand house near the town hall (Hôtel de Ville). The medieval cathedral itself seems almost too tiny for such a great man. Its pulpit arrogantly proclaims that Richelieu preached here – without saying precisely what gospel was preached by this courtier who so adroitly managed to combine service to the State with great office in the Church. The cathedral facade is Tuscan, a creation of the late seventeenth-century architect François le Duc, and its spire reaches 80 metres towards the heavens.

To discover, finally, a testimony to the finitude even of our religious aspirations, drive due southeast along the D949 and N148 from Luçon to Maillezais, by way of Fontenay-le-Comte. Fontenay-le-Comte is worth pausing for. Its main parish church, Notre-Dame, bears the characteristics of a seventeenth-century restoration by the 'Tuscan' François le Duc, who rebuilt its splendid steeple. The 'fountain of the four pipes' in the main square, created in 1542 by the master-mason Lienard de la Reau, carries a motto given to the town by François I: *'Felicium ingeniorum et scaturgio'* ('The source and fountain of happily gifted spirits'). That gifted spirit, the crime writer Georges Simenon, happily spent the period of the Nazi occupation here during World War II.

The road to Maillezais runs almost due south from Fontenay-le-Comte. In the year 1000 a converted Jew named Théodolin came here as prior to the Benedictine monastery and decided to rebuild it on a much more impressive scale. In the thirteenth century the monastery at Maillezais housed 200 monks and was served by countless villagers and local dependents. For 300 years its church was also the cathedral of the feudal bishops of the region. In the fifteenth century, when protestants dominated the town, their leader, Agrippa d'Aubigné, built the still impressive ramparts of Maillezais to protect his supporters. But all that

49

remains today of its monastery is a beautiful, deserted ruin.

The speediest route back to Nantes drives through Fontenay-le-Comte, turning right at Sainte-Hermine to take the N137 all the way to the city. The road passes through Chavagnes-en-Paillers and Montaigu on the way. Chavagnes-en-Paillers (just off the N137, to the left along the D6) was made famous by the parish priest Père Baudouin, who came here in 1801 when the town had been half-ruined by soldiers. He founded two teaching orders, the Ursulines of Jesus and the Daughters of Immaculate Mary, whose influence stretched far beyond the town. Chavagnes-en-Paillers still boasts two fine churches and a convent. Before the Revolution Montaigu could boast three churches and a convent – all gone – as well as a stronghold built by Louis IX, of which but a wall remains.

Further on the ravages of the Vendéen wars are subtly revealed by the fact that the churches at Saint-Hilaire-de-Clisson and Saint-Lumine-de-Clisson are both nineteenth-century buildings; but Saint-Lumine-de-Clisson happily preserves much of the fifteenth-century Château de la Courbe Jollière, with its massive, impressive towers.

Left **The eleventh-century cloisters which link the bishop's palace at Luçon to the early fourteenth-century abbey church and cathedral.**

Below **Rustic renaissance carving at Fontenay-le-Comte: note the closeness of the countryside – the windmill to the left, and the farm animals in the foreground.**

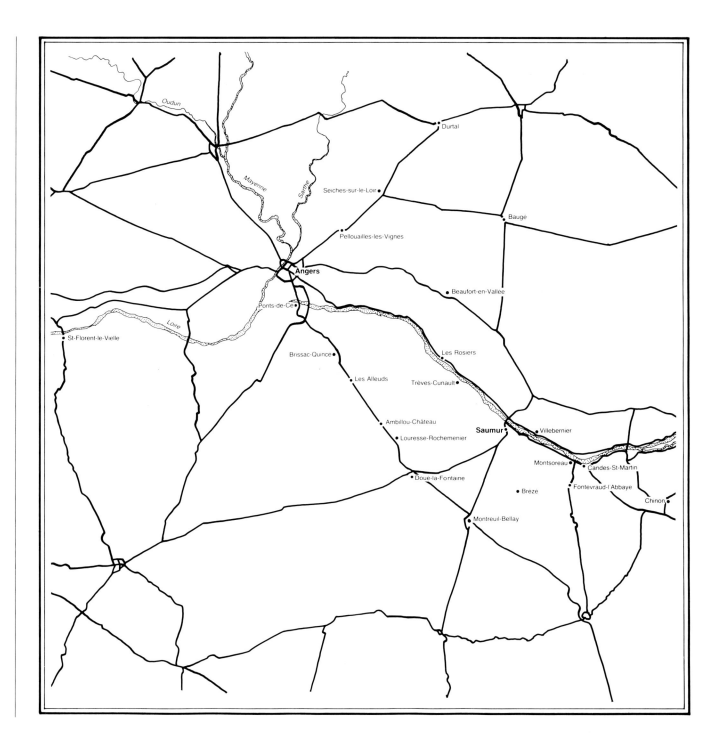

2
The Garden of France

Angers – Baugé – Beaufort-en-Vallée – Cunault –
Saumur – Fontevraud-l'Abbaye – Montreuil-Bellay
– Doué-la-Fontaine

The little town of Durtal, 34 kilometres northeast of Angers along the N23, has for centuries guarded the frontier of what is now the *département* of Maine-et-Loire. Its château was rebuilt in the sixteenth century and is now a peaceful hospice, but two fiercely machicolated towers remain as a reminder of its medieval past. You can visit the lovely buildings, admire the glazed earthenware medicine jars of the old pharmacy and look out over the lazy River Loir that flows by. The view is one that entranced the poet Paul Verlaine a century ago:

'For many years I lived in the best of châteaux,
In a most delicate country of animated water and
  hillsides',

he wrote. It is a description that fits the whole *département*.

Angers is the chief city of this land, once the capital of the duchy of Anjou, whose counts and dukes ruled here from the year 870. The grim walls of the château at Angers, with its great moat and drawbridge, still dominate the city, impressive and far more foreboding than the château at Durtal. At the entrance to the château, on the rock known as the World's End (*le bout du monde*), is the geographical centre of Angers, 25

metres above the lake of the Maine, where an orientation-table enables you to identify the glories of the southern part of the city spread out before you.

The castle at Angers is today named after the famous fifteenth-century Duke René, who was also King of Naples and Provence. Until this château was built in the late ninth century, the counts of Anjou lived in a palace close by the cathedral. Norman invaders forced them to create this more defensible home. In the twelfth century the Plantagenet count, Geoffrey le Bel, rebuilt the château, and the Capetian enemies of the Plantagenets demolished it. Between 1228 and 1238 Louis IX's queen, Blanche de Castille, built the present imposing mass, with no fewer than seventeen towers, made of stone and slate, and ramparts 900 metres long. The moat – 11 metres deep and 30 metres wide – is today a garden, and the fortress a tourist attraction. But for many years it was besieged, taken, retaken and several times threatened with destruction. At the end of the sixteenth century King Henri III ordered the complete demolition of the château, but its governor, Donadieu de Puycharic, liked the place too much and so delayed the work of destruction that only one-and-a-half floors of the towers were cut down. Then the château became a gaol; its defenders repulsed the

Exquisitely situated on the bank of the Loire west of Angers, the church of St Maurice at Chalonnes-sur-Loire has stood here since the eleventh century.

counter-revolutionary Vendéens in 1793; and now it is the property of the French Fine Arts Commission.

Medieval life in the château at Angers was by no means unremittingly brutal. In the 1370s, for instance, Louis I of Anjou commissioned a superb tapestry from the painter to the French court, Hennequin of Bruges. The Parisian artist Nicolas Bataille wove it; and Duke René bequeathed it to Angers Cathedral. The theme of the tapestry was the Apocalypse, illustrated in ninety scenes. In the eighteenth century few appreciated the worth of this tapestry and parts were damaged or lost. When it was put up for sale in 1843, the Bishop of Angers (Monsignor Angebault) had the foresight to buy what had once in fact belonged to his cathedral.

Since 1952, by arrangement with the cathedral authorities, the seventy-six surviving scenes have been displayed in specially constructed galleries inside the château. (The empty spaces where the missing panels ought to hang are intelligently filled with reproductions of paintings and miniatures depicting the originals.)

These must be among the finest tapestries in the world. The theme of the Apocalypse has been interpreted brilliantly by the great Flemish artist. The seven-headed dragon gives his sceptre to a multi-headed leopard. The same dragon menaces the Holy City. St Michael fights the dragon. A king with a long-bow, followed by a flying angel, rides a lovely white charger past a fruit tree, where sits a pretty bird. And these are not the only superb tapestries on display in the galleries of the château at Angers. There are tapestries in the fifteenth-century chapel of Sainte-Geneviève, which has a magnificent Angevin vault. My favourite of all the tapestries in the château is one woven in the sixteenth century depicting Penthésilée, queen of the Amazons. She stands in a beautiful flower-garden, a baton in her right hand, her left hand resting on a huge scimitar. In spite of her armour, her helmet, her long boots, she somehow remains entirely feminine, her skirt dividing to reveal a graceful leg, her face almost gentle. Elsewhere in these exquisite panels St Martin receives the blood of St Maurice (in little jars), and a noble lady plays a little organ in a garden in the presence of a boy and a long-haired, richly-dressed companion. Four superb panels depict the passion and resurrection of Jesus.

These great tapestries have inspired twentieth-century artists. Across the river, at No. 4, boulevard

Four of the seventeen grim towers in the ramparts of the château at Angers, overlooking the ornamental gardens planted on the site of the moat.

Arago, is the Hospital of St John (also called the Hôtel-Dieu). The English King Henry II founded this hospital in 1175. The great hall now houses not the sick but ten modern tapestries by Jean Lurçat, who died in 1966. He first saw the Apocalypse tapestries at Angers in 1938. They fired him to make a complementary series on the theme of the joy of life. After 1938 the traumas of twentieth-century warfare convinced Lurçat that life was altogether more severe, more bitter. His final theme was 'the song of the world'. He intended at his death to create more than ten tapestries, but the ones we have indicate the sombre depth of his vision, as well as the cataclysms and achievements of the twentieth century. Their themes are:

the terrible threat;
the man of Hiroshima;
the great charnel house;
the end of all things;
man in glory and peace;
water and fire;
champagne;
the conquest of space;
poetry;
and (the most enigmatic) ornamentos sagrados
    (sacred ornaments).

The hospital of St John is a rare example of late twelfth-century architecture. It has a particular connection with Britain since Henry II's purpose in founding it was partly to expiate the murder of Archbishop Thomas Becket. The main ward in which Lurçat's tapestries hang is over 22 metres wide, 60 metres long and 12 metres high. Fourteen graceful columns, with decorated capitals, divide the ward into three aisles. The vaulting is of that elegant high pattern peculiar to Anjou. Twenty-two more columns are built into its walls. Once over two hundred men and women were cared for here. Its old pharmacy is still in excellent order. The chapel dates from only slightly later than the great hall, and retains some of its original stained glass. The contemporary cloister is also wonderful; romanesque and barrel-vaulted, with a third side added by Jean de l'Éspine in the early sixteenth century.

Walk up the street behind the hospital to its ancient tithe barn. This magnificent building was restored in 1922, and its slate cellars now house a museum of wine, with antique bottles and old presses. Here the numerous convivial, bibulous meetings of the 'Confrerie des Chevaliers du Sacavin' take place in fancy dress to confer honours on members and to celebrate the glories of the wines of Anjou.

The members have much to celebrate. The western part of Anjou, for instance, being hilly and convoluted, offers farmers the opportunity of growing grapes on little slopes that present a different face to the sun at different seasons of the year, thus producing slight but clearly discernible variations in the taste of their wines. The best known is Rosé d'Anjou, grown all the way between Angers and Saumur to the southeast. The grapes – Gamay, Cot, Cabernet Franc and Groslot – are pressed intact, and the must is allowed to ferment for no more than a few hours, long enough to allow just the right pale pink to develop. Cabernet d'Anjou is a rosé even lighter in colour, lively and fruity. It, too, is created after soaking by a very rapid pressing, its special character in part due to the addition of the Sauvignon grape (or occasionally the grape known as Chardonnay).

To the south of Angers are grown the vines of the 'Coteaux-de-l'Aubance', which make a fine semi-dry white wine. The 'Coteaux-de-la-Loire' produce formidably fine whites, sometimes very dry, sometimes not, all perfect accompanying, say, duck à l'orange or a warm entrée. The cru known as 'Savennières' is regarded by the confraternity of the Chevaliers du Sacavin as the ideal partner for fish caught in the rivers of the region. As for reds, Anjou rouge is a relatively new appellation contrôlée, but good red wine has been drunk in these parts for centuries. Alexandre Dumas invented a totally believable character in his abbé of Angers who so excessively loved red wine that 'this magnificent cleric had become a purple abbé – the colour of the wine, so much of which his body had imbibed, as to have become incorruptible.' The best reds are produced round Saumur, but those grown in the Angers region are supple and charming, some of them giving off a beautiful flowery scent.

The ancient tithe barn of Angers lies to the north of the old quarter of Angers known as 'La Doutre'. Even further north along boulevard Arago is another reminder of the British connection with this part of medieval France, the thirteenth-century Tower of the English. The boulevard shortly becomes the D122 and leads to a grisly spot: the field of the martyrs, where 2000 people were put to death during the revolutionary terror of 1794.

A more entertaining walk is to explore the quarter of La Doutre. The grassy place de la Rochefoucauld between the hospital of St John and the river was laid out in the eighteenth century. South of the tithe barn is the place du Tertre from which a gentle stroll south leads to the old Benedictine abbey of Our Lady of la Ronceray. Foulques Nerra, Count of Anjou, founded this abbey in the eleventh century, though all but the church was rebuilt in the seventeenth. *Roncier* is French for thornbush, and the foundation was inspired by the miraculous discovery of a statue of the Virgin Mary in such a bush. Only noble women were admitted as members of the order. Many of them lost their lives at the Revolution. In the nineteenth century their abbey became first a hospital, then a warehouse and finally the school of arts and crafts. The seventeenth-century cloisters are magnificent. As for the abbey church, its round arches seem perilously flattened. The bronze Virgin is still in the crypt (entered from the church of the Holy Trinity next door). And a concert here is a magical experience.

Holy Trinity was founded by the sisters of Our Lady of la Ronceray. At the time of the Revolution the parish priest said that one consolation was that at least he was no longer bullied by nuns! It is a curious building, half romanesque, half gothic, the semi-circular bays and carved capitals belonging to the earlier style, the heavy pointed arches to the latter. A completely different style is that of the bell-tower, a masterpiece of Angevin renaissance architecture created by Jean de l'Éspine in 1540. Outside, the square (the place de la Laiterie) is delightful, surrounded by gabled houses. The most famous is the so-called 'house of Simon Poisson', its carvings representing science, freedom, magnificence, friendship and such virtues.

From the church of the Holy Trinity walk towards the river down rue Beaurepaire to find on your left an odd example of seventeenth-century charity: the famous Angers pawnshop, known as 'le mont de piété'. It was set up by an eighty-seven-year-old bishop of the city in 1684. 'The sole purpose of this establishment,' he wrote, 'is to help impoverished craftsmen of the city and its neighbourhood by providing them with interest-free loans.' His pawnshop was established in a fine fifteenth-century house. The charity prospered and gradually bought up surrounding buildings, including a couple of pretty towers bought from a group of nuns in 1723. The facade was superbly embellished. Inside is a monumental staircase with a thirteenth-century wrought-iron balustrade. The ceiling and beams were colourfully decorated. And needy citizens of Angers can still obtain a loan here.

Walk back past the church of the Holy Trinity and along boulevard Descazeaux to the Hôtel des Pénitentes. Its flamboyant facade is immediately recognizable to the left of the boulevard. The three dormer windows carry ostentatious, complicated gables. The tower is oddly fortified, for no one would think of attacking or defending such a building. Beside the tower is an arrogant door with two boastful turrets. Inside is a chimney built in the fantastic pattern of the sixteenth century, carved with grotesque heads and animals.

Above **The Château de Serrant at Saint-Georges-sur-Loire downstream of Angers, built from the sixteenth to the eighteenth centuries, takes all the features of a medieval fortress (such as the moat and tower) and transforms them into classical elegance.**

Right **The twin spires of Angers Cathedral flank the renaissance lantern which Jean de l'Éspine built in 1533 to house a bell weighing six tonnes. Both bell and cathedral are dedicated to the early Christian martyr St Maurice.**

The purpose of this house was bizarre. Marguerite Deshaies founded the Hôtel des Pénitentes in 1640 as a secure lock-up for women of ill-repute. Also accepted were fallen women who wanted a refuge from their former disreputable lives. This useful function was discontinued at the Revolution, when the house was transformed first into a women's prison and then into a courthouse. It now functions as a school of design.

A little street to the left of the Hôtel des Pénitentes leads into rue Saint-Nicolas, which you follow as far as the crossroads with two boulevards, across which rue Saint-Jacques leads to the abbey of St Nicolas the Poor. The site is a marvel of landscaping, the abbey itself mirrored in its own lake (once a quarry from which the stone of the château was dug). This watery connection is apposite. Foulques Nerra, sailing to Jerusalem, believed that Nicolas, the patron saint of mariners, had saved him from drowning in a terrible storm. He vowed to dedicate an abbey to the saint on his return to Angers. Monks of Marmoutier were brought here in 1020 when the abbey was finally built. They and their Benedictine successors became so rich that its dedication to an impoverished saint seemed scandalous. The buildings were sumptuously rebuilt in the first half of the eighteenth century, though the arcaded cloister and the ancient columns of the chapel still stand. The vicissitudes of history mean that this abbey has been in turn school, barn, barracks and military hospital. Today it is an old people's home. Next to it is a splendid park, a relatively recent creation (it was begun in 1937), harmonious and peaceful. It is hard to believe that in 1944 the Nazis executed sixty-six members of the French Resistance here.

This bank of the river offers a superb view of the château and cathedral of Angers. Cross the bridge of La Basse-Chaine and turn left behind the château to reach the cathedral. Angers Cathedral is dedicated to St Maurice, though the earliest church on this spot was dedicated to the Virgin Mary. The romanesque west porch boasts an impressive statue of Christ flanked by the symbols of the four evangelists, in an archway decorated with angels, saints and the twenty-four elders of the Apocalypse – all crying 'Allelujah'. Two elegant gothic spires surmount the facade, both early sixteenth century in date. Incongruously, almost comically, they flank an octagonal renaissance bell-tower added by Jean de l'Éspine in the 1530s.

Compared with the airy cathedral of Nantes, I find the interior of Angers Cathedral gloomy; but the dark sets off the stained glass to greater advantage, especially the late thirteenth-century lights in the choir. A brilliant, unsung local architect named André Robin created the rose windows in the north and south transepts, each quite different from the other. The woodwork and the organ case are all of the eighteenth century, splendid and chaste.

Between the cathedral of Angers and its château is an ancient quarter rivalling that of La Doutre across the river. Drapers and goldsmiths built fifteenth- and sixteenth-century mansions and palaces here, with magnificent wooden gates, towers and splendid gables. 'Doors embellished with enormous nails reveal the genius of our ancestors', wrote Honoré de Balzac, 'who traced above them domestic hieroglyphics whose meaning we shall never now decipher.'

North of the cathedral is a rich collection of lovely buildings. Pride of place is occupied by the bishops' palace, a strange stone and brick building, dating as far back as the twelfth century (it is one of the oldest secular houses in France), but deriving its present cloying romantic aspect from a nineteenth-century restoration. Inside, much remains of the earlier palace: a gorgeous fifteenth-century fireplace in the old granary; the twelfth-century crypt (now a chapel); the vast meeting-house, 30 metres long; the ceremonial staircase built by Bishop François de Rohan in 1510; and all resting on the old Gallo-Roman wall of Angers.

Close by stands the timbered 'Adam's House' in the place Sainte-Croix on the corner of the rue Montault. Anatole France used Adam's House as the setting of his novel *L'Orme du Mail* (*The Elm Tree on the Mall*). No one can say whether its name derives from the tree of life sculpted on its corner (which once must have carried statues of Adam and Eve), or from Judge Michel Adams who lived here in the eighteenth century. The bourgeoisie of Angers adored pomp and display, yet deplored paying house taxes, which were levied according to the area of ground covered by their homes – hence the building technique of overhanging gables, which Adam's House so well displays. What is more difficult to explain is why the two facades of this mansion are so strikingly different. One is pagan and classical, with hunting scenes, love-making and the fairy Melusine, half snake, half woman. The other is Christian, with carvings of saints and an allegory representing charity.

In rue Plantagenet, at No. 73, is the first town hall of Angers, the Hôtel de la Godeline, built in the early sixteenth century and much embellished in 1641. In the early sixteenth century Angers was in the pocket of a series of mayors all deriving from the Pincé family, and they commissioned Jean de l'Éspine to build their ostentatious, elaborately decorated Hôtel Pincé not far away at No. 32 rue Lenepveu. Civic arrogance preceded their downfall. In 1615 the current Pincé was jailed for unpaid debts and his mansions sold. In rue de Musée another powerful Angers family built the Logis Barrault at the end of the fifteenth century. Both the Logis Barrault and Hôtel Pincé are today art galleries. On holiday you can tire of art galleries, but the one in the Logis Barrault is certainly worth visiting to see the work of the local artist David d'Angers, especially his restrained yet tormented bust of Paganini.

Four churches and three gardens are also well worth visiting on this side of the river. The finest of the churches is the abbey of Saint-Aubin, the richest and oldest abbey of the city, founded in the mid sixth century and housing the venerable remains of its patron saint. The west door is stupendous, angels worshipping a hieratic, stern Madonna and Child, surrounded by saints and strange beasts. The rest of the abbey buildings are late seventeenth century and no less grand for that. As if this were not enough, the abbey is decorated with lovely medieval paintings and boasts an enormous bell-tower, 54 metres high.

The other three churches are Saint-Martin (in rue Saint-Martin, which leads directly northeast from the bell-tower of Saint-Aubin), with its remarkable twelfth-century arches and apse; the delicate thirteenth-century gothic Saint-Serge (southeast of the railway station); and the ruined abbey of All Saints (Abbaye de Toussaint), southwest of the cathedral along rue Toussaint.

The three gardens are the botanical garden where boulevard Saint-Michel meets boulevard Carnot, the arboretum of La Maulévrie just outside the city, and the colourful garden of 'Le Mail' in front of the town hall, where every Saturday an entrancing flower market is held. In southwest France I have my own plot of land that I am gradually turning into a garden, so I can go a long way to see what other gardeners have done in the past. Even so, the furthest of these three gardens, the arboretum, requires you to do no more than take the road to Ponts-de-Cé and just after you have left the city turn right into chemin d'Orgemont. The site is outside the city for (as the name Maulévrie indicates) the place was once a leper colony. It is now the headquarters of the Angers horticultural society, whose experimental garden is open to the public all the year round from 8 am. (It closes when the sun goes down or at 8.30 pm, whichever is earlier.)

But Angers has detained us too long. The N23 through Pellouailles-les-Vignes towards Durtal is a classic French road, straight, lined with lovely poplars. Pellouailles-les-Vignes lives up to its name as a centre for Anjou wines. But this is also a land producing luscious fruit: strawberries, peaches, raspberries, plums, cherries, apples and pears. 'Belle-angevine' is a particularly delicious pear from Angers. Vegetables grown in the region are equally sweet and tender.

Angers was the birthplace of the prince of gastronomes, Curnonsky. He was born Maurice-Edmund Sailland in 1872, and on first taking up journalism asked a friend to suggest a pen-name. The reply was, 'Why not "Sky"?' Sailland turned the reply into part Latin, 'Cur non Sky?' and that henceforth was his name. He grew to weigh nearly 130 kilos and died at the age of eighty-four (and then only through falling from an upstairs window).

Prince Curnonsky did not magnify the cuisine of the city of his birth beyond its merits. Angers today, like the rest of the Loire valley, has adopted the white butter sauce of the Nantais. But its kitchens produce straightforward honest food, what Curnonsky described as 'direct, reasonable, upright dishes which do not strive for effect'. Anjou, he added, 'is a paradise for peaceful digestion'. The fertile land around Pellouailles-les-Vignes helps to explain why.

Follow the N23 as far as Seiches-sur-le-Loir and turn right there to reach Baugé. Towards the year 1000 Foulques Nerra founded Baugé amidst this forest of pleasant glades interspersed with heather and broom. Here the château stands plump in its square, one gothic window indicating its small chapel and on the opposite flank a pretty renaissance doorway above which is the charming staircase turret. The whole building is plastered with a warm sandy mortar made from the local soil. Walk round the back where seven carved faces, medieval grotesques, peer down at you from another corner turret.

Duke René's mother, Yolande of Aragon, built the present château at Baugé in the fifteenth century. The duke himself greatly venerated one of the most famous

At Ecuillé, due north of Angers, Jean Bourré, minister of Louis XI, built the château of Plessis-Bourré with a sumptuousness (and a care for his own creature-comforts) unusual in the fifteenth century.

Statue of Joan of Arc at Baugé, where in fact her enemies the English had the best of the Hundred Years War and nearly ruined the surrounding countryside.

relics in France here, a golden figure of Jesus hanging on a cross fashioned with two cross-pieces and carved, it is said, out of wood from the actual cross on which he was crucified. Brought to Baugé by crusaders returning from Constantinople in the thirteenth century, this cross is now in the chapel of the Incurables, in rue de la Girouardière. When René married Isabelle of Lorraine, this relic was adopted by her house and became the pattern of the celebrated cross of Lorraine.

Immediately opposite the square of the château of Baugé you find the D60 which leads to Beaufort-en-Vallée, the town where, legend has it, Sir Lancelot of the Round Table was born. The beautiful fourteenth-century fortress from which Beaufort-en-Vallée

derives its name is now a picturesque ruin, and a place for a picnic with marvellous vistas of the surrounding countryside.

What I most marvel at in this small town is its crazily ornate parish church. This huge building spans nearly 45 metres between the transepts and 75 metres from east end to west. The bell-tower is as high as the transepts are wide, carrying five powerful bells of which the largest alone weighs 5500 kilos. Half of the church was built by the renaissance genius Jean de l'Éspine, and I must admit that his bits are the best. They include the bell-tower, the north transept and the lovely vaulting of the nave. Do not miss the little chapel next to the choir, built in honour of Jeanne de Laval, queen of Mayenne and a native of Beaufort-en-Vallée.

But the nineteenth-century architects who built the rest were as spirited a bunch as ever lived. They put the massive bells in de l'Éspine's tower. They built the main portal between 1869 and 1872. Since Nicolas Langouz of Angers had painted an *Adoration of the Magi* for the north transept in the seventeenth century, Jean-Michel Mercier matched it with his *St Augustine* in the nineteenth. During the Franco-Prussian War of 1870 peace was signed when enemy troops were barely 12 kilometres from Beaufort. With one accord the grateful citizens dedicated their south transepts (built between 1875 and 1876) to the Sacred Heart of Jesus. If the whole edifice does not quite equal the grandeur of Sacré-Cœur de Montmartre in Paris, it makes a laudable attempt. The stained glass by Édouard Didron alone cost 300,000 francs, and the great window of the Sacred Heart, commemorating the citizens' vow of 1870, was displayed at the Paris

A coiled metal snake glares balefully at the visitor to Beaufort-en-Vallée.

Universal Exhibition of 1889. The rest of the stained glass depicts scenes and legends from the life of the Virgin Mary, apart from two complementary windows, one of Joan of Arc – to represent the glory of France – the other of Jeanne de Laval – to represent the glory of Beaufort-en-Vallée. With deliberate pedantic inaccuracy, everyone in these nineteenth-century windows wears renaissance clothing!

From Beaufort-en-Vallée follow the signs to Les Rosiers (where there is a lovely old inn called *Porte de la Vallée*) and cross the River Loire to turn left along the D751 for Trèves-Cunault.

At Cunault is a masterpiece of romanesque architecture. Notre-Dame de Cunault is perhaps the longest romanesque church in western France – 70 metres altogether. This priory church was founded by

Fishing boats on the Loire at Le Thoureil, between Angers and Saumur, where the seductive peace and well-stocked river led monks to found an abbey in the sixth century.

Benedictine monks in the eleventh century. (The monks came from Saint-Philbert-de-Grand-Lieu in the Vendée.) Everything is stern here, including the imposing doorway topped by a tower and spire. Over this doorway sits a mutilated Madonna and Child, flanked by worshipping angels. Ten stone steps lead down into the nave. Inside the church is, surprisingly, a well, as well as wall-paintings of saints, martyrs, Christ himself, St Sebastian (bleeding profusely, though his hair is as yet undishevelled) and St Christopher crossing a river (fishes swimming around his feet, his stockings held up by a curious medieval suspender-belt). The capitals of 223 of the church's columns are carved and decorated with stories from the Bible and fantastic beasts. The church's other treasures include a thirteenth-century wooden shrine

containing the bones of St Maxenceul, a disciple of St Martin of Tours – bones that were already 800 years old when the shrine was constructed – and a sixteenth-century polychrome statue of Our Lady of Pity.

A little further on you reach Trèves, where the river bends (though sometimes in summer the Loire here seems more like sand-flats than a river). I find this an extremely pretty village, with a humble eleventh-century church by the river, white-walled houses, nooks and crannies and the ruins of a sixteenth-century château built by Robert Lemaçon, the chancellor of King Charles VII.

The River Loire is wider now, islands appearing from time to time in the middle, churches and châteaux dotted on either bank as the road curves following the course of the water. The finest of these châteaux is Boumois (on the other side of the Loire), which presents two faces to the world. One is gothic, dating from the end of the fifteenth century; the other is early renaissance, dating from the next century. Château Boumois is both a fortress and an elegant home. One of its delightful features is a large seventeenth-century pigeon-house, well preserved in its original condition.

Suddenly ahead is the great château of Saumur – in a sense no different from the rest, only larger – with its pepper-pot towers, its elegant bays, its bleak walls. It is best seen, I think, from the other side of the blue river in the lush green of early June, say from close by the village of Villebernier. Guy Geoffroy, Count of Poitiers, burned the château down at the beginning of the eleventh century, and it was rebuilt in the twelfth and fourteenth. The citizens of Saumur rightly boast that their château seems to spring directly out of a medieval manuscript, since it appears in the miniature

Inside the church at Trèves, four fearsome heads repel evil spirits from the baptismal waters of the romanesque font.

Right **The fourteenth-century château at Saumur, with its twin towers (nicknamed 'Grenetière' and 'Papegault') and the remains of its once powerful walls.**

illustrating the month of September in the *Très Riches Heures* of the Duc du Berry.

Saumur is altogether charming, particularly the irregular place Saint-Pierre when the Sunday morning flea market is in full swing. The market spills down neighbouring streets as far as the riverside and along to the place de la République, and I have picked up many an old book-bargain here. Half-timbered houses sport classical dormer windows, matched and more than matched by the classical facade of St Peter's Church.

The first time I ever went into St Peter's, Saumur, I had been so long detained by the delights of the flea market that the church was about to close. An obviously authoritative parishioner, kindly postponing his Sunday lunch, got hold of the keys from the priest and proudly showed me round. He had much to be proud of: not only the Angevin gothic vaulting of the nave, but also the splendid nineteenth-century panelling backing the high altar, and the sixteenth-century stalls and misericords (with delightful scenes incorporating humans and beasts).

My unknown guide showed me a baptismal font made of porphyry dating from 1662; quaint stone medallions half-way up the walls of the nave; gentle lierne vaulting in a sixteenth-century side chapel which you approach through an arrogant renaissance arch; the seventeenth-century organ-case with its comical cherubs; and most proudly of all, the early sixteenth-century tapestries on display in this church. These tapestries depict the life of St Peter and the life of St Florent, missionary-disciple of St Martin of Tours. (He founded the monastery of Saint-Florent-le-Vielle between Angers and Nantes.) The tapestry depicting

---

The town of Saumur was consistently faithful to the kings of France from the twelfth century. Only when its protestant governor lost his fortune were the old fortifications dismantled.

Peter's crucifixion is no greater than any of the others, I suppose, but it is the one I nowadays always return to look at first. A bald man in boots kneels to hammer a nail into Peter's left hand. Everyone is in sixteenth-century clothing, except the saint himself, who has a rope tied around the bottom of his robe to stop it falling about his ears (for of course he is being crucified upside-down).

My guide locked the church but insisted on showing me one other fascinating fact about it. At the time of the Revolution St Peter's was declared no longer a Christian church but a temple of reason. We walked to the end of rue Fourrier where he showed me the inscription: 'rue du Temple de la Raison'.

Rue Duplessis-Mornay (named after the great Huguenot leader of Saumur) leads to the château, through winding, well-restored medieval houses. Devotees of horse-racing will warm to the château's equestrian museum, whose most bizarre exhibit is the skeleton of Flying Fox, winner of the Derby in 1899, and the most touching a plaque commemorating over one million of these innocent beasts killed by both sides during World War I. The town is graced by a school of cavalry which presents a celebration of equestrian skills each July.

Saumur was an important centre in megalithic times and a couple of kilometres south, in the suburb of Bagneux, is one of the best-preserved megalithic dolmens in the Loire valley: a 30 metres long tunnel, $3\frac{1}{4}$ metres high and $7\frac{1}{2}$ metres wide, made of sixteen standing and four table stones, and running northeast/southwest.

Leave Saumur by driving southeast along quai Carnot. You pass the gothic town hall with its delicate curly shallow columns abutting onto a castellated fortress and then drive along quai Mayaud towards Chinon, past the pilgrim church of Notre-Dame-de-Ardilliers. This early sixteenth-century building was added to by the generosity of Richelieu a hundred years after its foundation, and by Mme de Montespan

(Louis XIV's mistress from 1670 to 1679), who paid for the dome in 1695. Attacking Saumur in 1940 German bombers all but demolished the church, which has been beautifully restored.

This fecund land seems to grow statues of saints as well as succulent grapes and fruits. The word 'Ardilliers' attached to the church of Notre-Dame is a *patois* version of *argileux*, or clayey soil. In the Middle Ages a farmer came across a statue of the Virgin Mary miraculously planted on this spot. Another medieval statue of the Virgin, made of blackened wood, was found in a field of lentils near Saumur. *Patois* for lentils is *nantilles*, and south of the château in Saumur along rue Duruy stands the twelfth-century church of Notre-Dame-de-Nantilly. The gorgeous flamboyant south aisle was a gift to the church by King Louis XI.

Outside Saumur the D947 is flanked by fantastic old troglodyte dwellings and a troglodyte church. Advertisements remind you that you can stop and buy Saumur wines, invariably an excellent drink. Two *appellations contrôlées*, 'Saumur' and 'Coteaux-de-Saumur', are fruity white wines. This region grows little sweet or semi-sweet wine; but it does nurture excellent grapes that produce little-known reds and rosés. 'Champigny' is said to be a red that ages well, though I have never kept a bottle long enough to know. The whites tend to curl delightfully on your tongue, their agreeable suppleness largely derived from the grape Chinon. Altogether some thirty communes produce 'Saumur' wines, so that variations in taste can be quite distinct. But what one producer (VUL of Saumur) puts on his bottles can be applied to many a vintage here: 'Our wines make the ladies wink their eyes and give the men spirit.'

Along this stretch of the Loire the wines are matured in cellars dug out of the chalky tufa (the same material that hardens into the lovely white stone of the buildings), the must of the caves, I like to imagine, giving its own nuance to the taste of Saumur wines. Increasingly, too, the vignerons are producing a sparkling Saumur fermented in the fashion of champagne.

Salmon from the Loire, delicious shad (braised in Saumur wine) and the potted meats (if that is remotely a decent translation of *rillettes*) for which the kitchens of Saumur are renowned, mean that you should not be in too great a hurry to drive on, unless your plan is to eat in one of the restaurants of Montsoreau, 11 kilometres of entrancing riverside drive east from Saumur.

Alexandre Dumas' novel *La Dame de Monsoreau* has invested Montsoreau with an eternally glamorous patina of sensuality, embellishing the tale of the countess whose lover, Bussy d'Amboise, was lured to his death in 1579 at the hands of her husband while supposing himself to be keeping an assignation with his mistress. (Dry as dust historians say that these events, or something like them, took place not here but at Château de Coutancière on the other side of the river.) Jean de Chambes, ancestor of the man who so viciously avenged his wife's infidelities, rebuilt the château of Montsoreau in the fifteenth century. The renaissance staircase tower is a later addition, notable for a carving of two monkeys raising rocks by means of a pulley, fortified by the motto, 'I shall make it.'

The château of Montsoreau fascinates me because of its impregnable strategic position, overlooking the confluence of the Loire and the Vienne, far more than it does because it now houses the museum of the 'Goums', i.e. those Moroccan soldiers who fought for their French colonial conquerors. The two rivers actually meet at Candes-Saint-Martin, 1½ kilometres southeast of Montsoreau. St Martin of Tours died here in the year 397, and the effigy of a bishop in the northeast chapel of Candes church marks the spot where he breathed his last earthly breath. It hardly

The confluence of the Rivers Vienne and Loire at Montsoreau.

needs saying that he did not die in the thirteenth-century church but in a little house that once occupied this sacred spot.

From Montsoreau and Candes-Saint-Martin the D947 south skirts the Fontevraud forest, which in olden times was called 'cut-throat' (*tranche-col*) forest since few who ventured through it came out the other side. Fontevraud itself is named after a legendary brigand chief, Évrault, who came across a powerful missionary preacher named Robert d'Arbrissel asleep in these dangerous woods. Évrault brought his band of cut-throats to make sport with Robert, who instead awoke and converted them all to the Christian faith.

The abbey of Fontevraud (the town is also called Fontevraud-l'Abbaye) is where two of the most illustrious English kings, and two great, suffering English queens lie buried.

Their last resting-place is a superb early twelfth-century church, with enormous columns topped by elaborate carved capitals. Delay seeking out the sculpted royal tombs in order to enthuse over these lovely buildings, which once housed a double monastery of men and women. (Thirty-six abbessess successively ruled both sexes at Fontevraud.) They obviously ate well, for the early twelfth-century octagonal kitchen (now called the Tour d'Évrault) reminds one of its famous twin at Glastonbury in England and is to my mind even more entrancing. Its eight hearths at one time cooked for 5000 persons, attached in one way or another to the abbey. The daughters of King Louis XV used to play in the lovely sixteenth-century cloisters where once the religious studied and meditated. The romanesque refectory of the convent was given its fine pointed vault in the same century. I have rarely seen such a fantastic

The old, dangerous 'cut-throat' forest of Fontevraud has become an orderly, well-cultivated and entrancing wood.

The lovely village of Candes-Saint-Martin, whose vineyards flank the River Loire and where St Martin of Tours died in 397.

chapter-house, beautifully arched, the walls sumptuously tiled, the floor puritanically decorated in black and white lozenges. And until the Revolution Fontevraud-l'Abbaye prospered and expanded, so that its remaining buildings constitute the most extensive religious house to be seen in France today. The medieval gardens have been carefully restored. Although part of the abbey is now a prison, visitors are still welcome, provided you go to the right entrance.

The sovereigns buried here constitute an extraordinary dynasty. Henry II of England (1154–89) lies sculpted in stone beside his wife Eleanor of Aquitaine. She was the daughter of the Count of Poitou and had been a wife once already by the time she married Henry. Being a distant relative of her first husband, King Louis VII of France, their tempestuous marriage

was eventually annulled, and within two months Eleanor was married again and crowned Queen of England in Westminster Abbey. The patrimony of husband and wife was immense, she bringing the disputed heritage of Aquitaine, he not only the future kingdom of England but also the dukedom of Normandy and lordship over Anjou and Maine. Their relationship was stormy. For some years Henry had Eleanor imprisoned. But after his death she was a superb regent of England. She came to Fontevraud to die. Her tomb depicts her as unusually quiet, apparently reading a godly book. Her dead husband clutches the sceptre that he no longer wields.

The son she loved best was Richard the Lionheart. Besieging Châlus near Limoges to the south in 1199 he was mortally wounded by an arrow shot from the castle walls. His mother was with him as he lay a long time dying. He lies close by her in a sculpted stone tomb in the abbey of Fontevraud. His death did not ease the succession to the English throne. Eleanor's fourth son, John, had already unsuccessfully conspired to take the English crown from Richard the Lionheart. Richard planned as his successor his nephew Arthur of Brittany, but John was sharp enough to murder Arthur and become king instead.

John abducted and married Isabelle d'Angoulême, the fourth member of this English dynasty to lie in Fontevraud. The abduction was the pretext for Philippe Auguste of France to have John's French territories confiscated by his peers. King John died in 1216 and Isabelle, who lived on till 1246, became a nun at Fontevraud l'Abbaye, where she now lies in her lovely wooden tomb. For many centuries the British claimed her tomb as well as those of Richard the

The seventeenth- and eighteenth-century domestic quarters of the former abbey at Fontevraud contrast with the stern tower of the romanesque abbey church behind.

Lionheart, Henry II and Eleanor. Exploiting her friendship with Napoleon III's wife Eugénie, Queen Victoria almost managed their transfer to Britain, but the fall of the Third Empire in 1870 aborted the plan, one of the more beneficent effects of the Franco-Prussian War.

Drive now due west from Fontevraud to Brézé, through more Saumur-Anjou vineyards. Brézé is oddly dominated by its early twentieth-century church spire, which is less of a joy the closer you approach it. The well-restored sixteenth-century château, some distance from the village, is much nicer. But for a rare treat hasten southwest towards Montreuil-Bellay on the little River Thouet.

As befits such a treat, you do not at first realize what is in store, so banal is the new part of the town. The old town is partially enclosed in thirteenth-century walls. The fifteenth-century château overlooks the river, with arches, turrets, crenellations and a wondrous defensive church. Hostile to the outside world, even its windows open only half-way up. The precautions paid off. Four other churches in Montreuil-Bellay were destroyed during the Wars of Religion and at the Revolution. This huge collegiate church of Notre-Dame, endowed to support a whole chapter of clergy, survived. Impregnable behind its château walls, it is approached through a great pointed arch (rebuilt in the nineteenth century, as if churches then were still at risk) and by a bridge across a now empty moat, across which parishioners could come to worship without disturbing or gaining access to the great ones inside the great house.

Notre-Dame of Montreuil-Bellay is 44 metres long, over $12\frac{1}{4}$ metres wide and 18 metres high. Its west facade is powerful, incorporating a pointed porch, a double door and a rose window. The style of the whole church is technically called ogival-Plantagenet. On the left wall is a private chapel to separate the worshipping seigneurs from their underlings. You notice what seems a great blemish on the walls – a dour black band

Left It is hard to judge whether this elaborate corner of the château at Brézé owes more to its nineteenth-century restorer than to its original builders.

Below As the renaissance blossomed in France, lords and ladies transformed parts of their grim châteaux into elegant homes, as in this delicious wing of the fortress at Montreuil-Bellay.

painted high up round three sides of the building. Its purpose was to lament the death of the noble persons of Montreuil-Bellay, whose armorial bearings are painted against this black background. The fourth side of the church is its apse, with niches for a series of saintly statues, of which six, made of gilded plaster, remain.

Foulques Nerra began building the château here in the eleventh century. In the fifteenth the local lords of Harcourt rebuilt it, retaining the old towers and the double walls, and the lovely statue of the Virgin Mary in a niche over the main entrance. Altogether no fewer than six drum towers guard the old château and a late fifteenth-century hospice of the knights of St John (now an old people's home). Inside the hospice chapel, shaped like a Latin cross, two stern ranks of columns separated worshipping women from worshipping men. Incidental delights are recently restored wall-paintings depicting St Roch, St Andrew and St Sebastian.

The defensive aspect of the château of Montreuil-Bellay has left an unexpected bonus for the twentieth-century visitor. It perches high above the river, and its tree-lined gardens offer a splendid panorama across the water. The air of peace about the whole town ought not to blind us to its sometimes violent past. The Plantagenets and the kings of France fought to possess the town. So did Huguenots and Catholics, followed by revolutionaries and Vendéens. Here in 1828 Victor Hugo's friend Devalle was killed in a duel, aged only twenty-eight. The walls surrounding the town are vicious enough, especially at porte Saint-Jean, where balls of stone set into the round towers were designed

Here the château at Montreuil-Bellay presents its more formidable aspect, initially built to dominate the River Thouet (and restored in the nineteenth century as a dream château of gothic France).

to repulse projectiles in perilously unpredictable directions.

Eventually, however, in our own century, para-doxically one that has been as savage as any, peace is exuded by Montreuil-Bellay. Two disused houses of God contribute to this gentle ambience. The former chapel of the Augustinians is no longer needed by the Church and has been colonized by a group of local craftsmen who will sell you translucent lamps and elaborately ornate wax candles. Outside the town walls are the ruins of the twelfth-century abbey of Nobis, situated where the River Thouet provided water for the monks' kitchen, to mingle with their wine, and for their daily ablutions. Here the locals have provided their visitors with seats, tables and a children's playground. The abbey itself affords a splendid view of the château. You must bring your own food for a picnic.

Take the D761 northwest to Doué-la-Fontaine. Doué rightly assumes the title 'city of roses', exporting three million rose bushes a year. As for 'la Fontaine', the name derives from a tremendous rectangular basin dug out of the rock in 1767, into which jets of water continually play. But Doué is much older than this. The Romans, it is said, built a mini-arena here, with an underground entrance and stepped seats that still stand. Curmudgeonly scholars claim that this arena is nothing more than a medieval quarry adapted for open-air theatre (which, if true, is in itself remarkable enough). The gardening citizens of Doué-la-Fontaine have enterprisingly transformed this scene of mortal combat (or medieval quarry and playhouse) into a charming little park. I should like to ask the curmudgeonly historians why medieval quarrymen could not have delved in what was once a Roman theatre. Roman remains have, after all, been disco-vered elsewhere in Doué-la-Fontaine, in the fifteenth-century church of Saint-Denis for instance. My own view is that most features of any landscape or town are older than nearly anyone realizes.

Above The 'arena' at Doué-la-Fontaine: originally either a Roman amphitheatre or a medieval quarry; today a delightful garden.

Right The entrancing architectural mixture at Château Brissac is due to the sudden impoverishment of Marshal Charles de Cossé, who would otherwise have pulled down the two fourteenth-century round towers and replaced them in a style matching the rest.

An interesting modern feature of Doué-la-Fontaine is its unusually humane zoo (well signposted), created in 1961 by Louis Gay. Monsieur Gay was determined that, insofar as this was possible for animals cooped up in the Loire valley, each species in his zoo should live freely and naturally. Serpents, pythons, bison, kangaroos, vultures and boa-constrictors are but a few of the hundreds of species happily roaming (more or less) the grottoes, cages and galleries covering four hectares of parkland.

From Doué-la-Fontaine a good road leads directly northwest back to Angers. You could stop again and again: at Louresse-Rochemenier with its troglodyte houses and its museum of troglodytism; at Ambillou-Château, where the château in question was built between the thirteenth and the fifteenth centuries, and where there is an ancient windmill that still works and an even older parish church; and at Les Alleuds, where the lake was dug by monks and where the church of their former priory should make any tourist pause. But our aim is Brissac-Quincé.

The Brézé family built themselves a château at Brissac in the eleventh century, but since then it has been considerably altered, with additions and bits pulled down and rebuilt, so that of their medieval home only the fourteenth-century towers still stand. Most of the present château was built in the early seventeenth century. The man who rebuilt it, Charles de Cossé, Marshal of France, would have demolished every ancient part had he not happily run out of cash. In consequence of his lack of money, the lovely facade is entrancingly asymmetrical. Its pitted walls are constructed out of long narrow bricks, the cornices and mouldings out of stone. Five classic orders of architecture embellish its main facade. One tower is comically topped with a dumpy cap, as though someone had put a hat of tiles on its head and squashed it down. I both salute his architect (who was called Jacques Corbineau) and pity him, the first emotion for his achievement in rebuilding much of the château at Brissac-Quincé, the second for his fortunate inability to rebuild everything.

The church, high up in the village, is built in much the same style as the château (transformed ecclesiastically) and out of the same materials. The stones are growing a darker brown now, akin to those of Angers. To the north side of Brissac-Quincé church stands its strange tower and spire. Many bits of medieval tracery have clearly been removed from the windows, replaced by renaissance mullions. The apse is glorified by beautifully-coloured renaissance glass.

And now it is time to drive back to Angers, passing as we do the old ramshackle windmill of Brissac-Quincé, a reminder that Anjou possesses more of these venerable sources of power than almost any other part of France.

Many disused windmills in the Loire valley, such as this one south of Angers, have been converted into picturesque private homes.

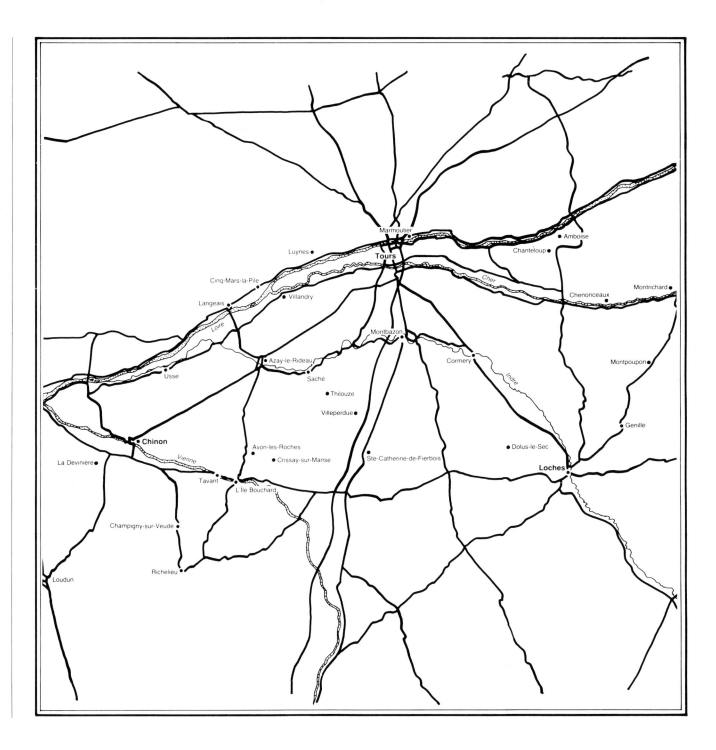

3
Poets and Princes

Tours – Luynes – Langeais – Azay-le-Rideau –
Tavant – Richelieu – Chinon – Amboise –
Chenonceaux – Loches

Honoré de Balzac was born at Tours in 1799 and he set his novel *Le Lys dans la vallée* (*The Lily of the Valley*) in the Touraine. A romantic tragedy, it begins with the young Félix de Vandenesse, after a childhood as deprived of affection as Balzac's own, taking part in a ball given at Tours by the Duke of Angoulême. There he meets an unknown woman of captivating beauty, kisses her (in spite of her own protests and almost in spite of himself) and falls passionately, platonically in love. When he quixotically takes an English aristocratic lady as mistress in Paris, the woman of Tours dies of misery.

Balzac's novel is full of entrancing descriptions of this region, for Félix de Vandenesse goes to live in a château by the side of the River Indre, between Montbazon and Azay-le-Rideau, a land of 'châteaux set amidst hills, where in a lovely sweep of emerald the Indre winds like a serpent'. Félix broods on his love each day, leaning against a walnut tree, while the windows of the cottages and the slate roofs of houses shimmer in the haze of the midday sun.

Balzac returned to Tours and its region in his novel *La Femme de trente ans* (*A Woman of Thirty*). The little River Cisse also seemed to him like a serpent, 'gilded in the sun, twisting and turning through the emerald-green of the meadows in spring', while the majestic Loire itself sported little mid-stream islands, like jewels on a necklace. The city of Tours itself seemed to Balzac to rise straight out of the waters, its old cathedral towers reaching up to the sky.

Tours rises from two rivers, the Loire to the north and the Cher to the south. The Gauls built a town called Altionus on the right bank of the Loire and the Romans extended it across to the left bank, changing its name to Caesarodunum. Christianity was preached here in the third century by St Gatien, to whom the cathedral is dedicated, and then by the famous soldier-saint Martin.

Martin was born in Pannonia by the River Danube. His famous act of costly charity, slicing his cloak in two to give one half to a naked beggar, was done while he was still a soldier in the Roman legion and before he had been baptized a Christian. After his own conversion to Christianity all his instincts were to retire as far as possible from the world into monasticism. He founded a monastery in Poitou, but in 371 was forced very much against his will to accept consecration as Bishop of Tours. He refused to live in a fine house, preferring caves outside the city.

Even then Martin continued to found new religious

houses, in particular the great monastery at Marmoutier. To visit Marmoutier today (only 3 kilometres north across the modern motorway bridge) is to be offered a unique insight into the early medieval Christian mind. After the Normans had devastated the first monastic buildings at Marmoutier, Benedictine monks rebuilt them. Here in 1092 Pope Urban II preached the first Crusade. The abbey continued to flourish until the Revolution, and then was sold by the republicans and virtually destroyed. Only the fortified ramparts and one medieval doorway remained of what had once been one of the greatest treasures of the Touraine. In 1847 monks of Sacré-Cœur in Paris bought the property and rebuilt a monastery here. Today their successors will show visitors around the old Benedictine remains and also the remarkable underground cells of their earliest predecessors (afternoons only).

When St Martin died at Candes near Chinon in 397, the Christians of Tours snatched his sacred body back and buried him under an oratory outside the city. (A stained-glass window at Candes shows the thieves from Tours stealing Martin's corpse.) Two centuries later his fame was spread throughout Christendom by the great historian and Bishop of Tours, St Gregory. A humble oratory was now considered far from sufficient to house St Martin's illustrious bones, and the first of several great basilicas was constructed to honour them with the dignity they deserved. Gregory proudly expatiated on its dimensions: 'In length the church is a hundred-and-sixty feet, and in breadth sixty; the distance from ground to the roof is forty-five feet; there are thirty-two windows around the altar and twenty in the nave.' The whole building, he wrote, has a hundred-and-twenty columns and eight towers. Martin's saintly relics rested here in peace until the Wars of Religion, when the protestants of Tours seized them, burned them and threw his ashes to the winds.

By the fifth century 20,000 people lived in this city.

The Visigoths coveted Tours and took it in 473. The founder of the Frankish dynasty, Clovis, took it back again, was baptized on the feast of St Martin, 498, and made Martin's episcopal city the national shrine of his kingdom.

In spite of the depredations of the Normans, this important cross-roads (by this time known as Urbs Turonum) continued to flourish throughout the Middle Ages, as did the monastery founded here by St Martin. The saint's miracle-working remains made both monastery and city famous centres of pilgrimage, and the main pilgrims' way from Saint-Denis in Paris to Santiago de Compostela in Spain passed through Tours.

In the eighth century, Alcuin, the famous English scholar and adviser of Charlemagne, became abbot of the monastery Martin had founded at Tours and created a renowned school of philosophy and theology here – the first in France. Soon the kings of France made the city their home, and in consequence Tours was the centre of much of the fighting between English and French during the Hundred Years War. Some protection was given by the great wall which the citizens had flung around their city in the thirteenth century. Although many churches (including the cathedral) were pillaged by the Huguenots during the Wars of Religion, the catholics of Tours seized power again, rebuilt them and incidentally managed to put to death a good number of their protestant opponents in revenge. Silk spun at Tours became famous and extremely profitable, and in the seventeenth century a second ring of walls had to be built around a city that in 400 years had doubled in size.

Much, alas, was destroyed in World War II. The retreating French did a fair amount of the damage themselves, blowing up part of the eighteenth-century Pont Wilson, for example. The Germans did the rest. The war left most of the city in ruins and 9000 citizens dead.

I often think that Tours has been rebuilt as an

exasperating mess, but in truth there is much to see here and the people are charming (Balzac described them as 'artistic, poetic, vigorous and extremely reticent in expressing their innermost feelings'). The city has regained its old prosperity. Large modern quarters and industrial suburbs have sprung up around the restored ancient quarter. Pont Wilson, which is over 430 metres long, is today an excellent example of civic pride, for it was beautifully rebuilt in its original mid eighteenth-century style, after the floods of 1978 had demolished another four piers.

The cathedral, dedicated to St Gatien, was built between 1220 and 1547, resolutely refusing to make up its mind which style of architecture should predominate. I like the rose windows of the transepts very much; the stained glass is splendid, especially the fifteen tall windows in the choir, dating from the middle of the thirteenth century (and including a fine Tree of Jesse); but I do not find the interior so inspiring as that of the cathedral at Angers. This does not mean that it is not wonderful! Well worth seeking out is the white marble tomb of two chubby-cheeked children of Charles VIII and Anne of Brittany, the eldest son wearing his crown. This tomb was sculpted for the first chapel south of the choir in the very early sixteenth century. Then look west, especially when the setting sun is gleaming through the intricate tracery of the windows.

The west facade of Tours Cathedral is lovely, a rare example of an extremely successful monumental piece of flamboyant architecture. Alas, few of the statues destroyed by the Huguenots in 1562 have been replaced. A couple of towers crown the whole, refusing (in the fashion of this cathedral) to match each other perfectly. To add to the stylistic confusion (which is, I must add, not at all displeasing), the towers are topped by a couple of renaissance cupolas.

On the north side of the cathedral is the former choir school, known as 'La Psalette'. Again the architecture is pleasingly varied: a flamboyant gallery dating from

the 1440s, and the north and east wing from the early sixteenth century. La Psalette houses a unique fifteenth-century bishop's library, as well as a splendid spiral staircase in the northeast tower. Walk on to the terrace for a breathtaking view of the flying buttresses of the north transept of the cathedral.

South of Tours Cathedral is the former bishop's palace, which became a museum of fine arts at the Revolution. Its contents are a rich collection drawn from local châteaux and abbeys as well as judiciously bought by the city. One of my favourite paintings was brought here as booty from Italy during the Napoleonic wars: Mantegna's *Resurrection*, a master-

Michel Colombe, who died at Tours in 1512, sculpted by François Sicard (in the place François-Sicard). Colombe was the last great gothic sculptor of France (and his masterpiece is the tomb of François II of Brittany and Margaret de Foix in Nantes Cathedral).

piece of audacious perspective. (It once was the left-hand side of a decorated panel behind the altar in the church of San Zeno, Verona.) The museum possesses a second part, *Jesus disguised as the gardener*. The third wing of this triptych is in the Louvre. Another entrancing work of art in the museum is a statue of Diana hunting, sensually modelled by Jean-Antoine Houdon in 1776. And the palace itself happens to be a work of art as well. One room, for instance, la salle Louis XIII, boasts a delightful wooden chimney carved with four caryatids.

The massive building will either overwhelm visitors with its crude power or strike aesthetes as irredeemably vulgar. (I number myself among the first group.) The basilica in rue des Halles in which St Martin's sacred relics lay was rebuilt many times, finally (so far) in the nineteenth century. Of the old romanesque basilica, only two towers, known as the tour de Charlemagne and the tour de l'Horloge (the one with the dome) still stand, to illustrate the folly of destroying the rest. Next to them was built a nineteenth-century basilica, in the Roman-Byzantine style, with an imposing dome. The architect was Victor Laloux. (Laloux also built the railway station in 1895.) While the new basilica was still building, that enterprising British tourist T. Frederick Bumpus visited Tours. 'To the sumptuous but as yet incomplete modern basilica of St Martin, a satisfactory visit was paid' early one morning, he recorded. It was, he observed, with the exception of Sacré-Cœur-de-Montmartre, 'perhaps the costliest and most imposing of modern French basilicas.' Then he wrote a lament for the old church:

'All that remains of the once far-famed abbey are the clock and Charlemagne towers. These noble masses, which formerly stood at the northeast and southwest angles of the nave, are now separated by one of the principal and busiest streets in Tours, which traverses the entire site of the nave, and beyond them not a trace remains of this large and time-honoured church which for the alleged reasons of superfluity and needless expense was destroyed during the early years of the present century, having survived the shock of the Revolution.'

A visit to the late nineteenth-century basilica of Saint-Martin in Tours is in my view essential, at least the first time you are in Tours. Its dome is impressive. The marble pulpit is modelled on that at Messina. The crypt, containing a replica of St Martin's tomb, is sustained by great red piers of granite. And close by is the market square (though I must here also recommend the flower market held every Wednesday and Saturday along boulevard Béranger, west of the totally delightful neo-classical town hall – Laloux's work, between 1896 and 1904 – and the mid nineteenth-century law courts).

For a glimpse of medieval Tours you must visit the church of Saint-Julien on the south bank of the Loire, where rue Colbert meets rue Nationale. St Gregory of Tours founded an abbey here, but the church we see today – a very satisfying blend of romanesque and early gothic – dates from the mid thirteenth century. (The previous church was destroyed by a hurricane in 1225, leaving only the old bell-tower and main porch fit to be incorporated in the new one.) Some of the romanesque capitals of the columns inside the church of Saint-Julien are quite powerful; seek out especially a naked fellow hanging upside-down, his legs already chewed by grimacing demons, a carving that expresses to me all the terror that beset medieval man.

The courtyard of the former abbey leads down into the monks' gently vaulted cellars. These thirteenth-century cellars today house the museum of Touraine wines. The wines of Touraine always seem to me stronger, with a touch more body, than most other wines of the Loire valley. The climate helps. Summers here are often exceptionally warm (almost always too hot for me in August); winters are usually extremely mild; and even at the very end of the grape harvest the warm weather seems to allow more and more luscious late grapes to ripen. Wines from the Coteaux-du-Loir-Jasnières are produced north of Tours. Other *appellations contrôlées* are Touraine itself, Touraine-Amboise, Touraine-Mesland and Touraine-Azay-le-Rideau – all four producing red, white and rosé wines. Two more red wines of this region are Chinon and Saint-Nicolas-de-Bourgueil, both made from the Cabernet Franc grape, and a fine white (even though the soils of Touraine generally favour reds) is Vouvray. The grape that creates Vouvray is the Chenin Blanc, grown north of the River Loire close by Tours. Both Vouvray and Montlouis (grown south of the river) are whites from Touraine that are often transformed, in the fashion of champagne, into excellent sparkling wines.

I adore crayfish, and cooked in this wine in the restaurants of Tours *écrevisses au vouvray* are indescribably beautiful. I am not so fond of *andouillette vouvrillonne*, since I have no relish for small sausages made of chitterlings, but I have seen many Frenchmen avidly tucking into them in and around Tours. Restaurants here also deliciously mix fruit with meats and poultry, for instance pork or duck with prunes (*porc aux pruneaux*; *canard aux pruneaux*). The best chefs will have soaked the prunes overnight in a dry Vouvray. *Porc aux pruneaux* is often served with a sauce that exudes the savour of red-currant jelly and rich cream. I do not know why the pigs of Touraine are particularly succulent, but potted pork *rillettes* are a famous speciality of the region. The chefs of Touraine also succulently combine tender cuts of veal with the more expensive mushrooms (such as *mignon de veaux aux morilles*), for the caves in which the wines of Touraine mature are often dank enough to sport the finest fungi. Often some of these are served on toast, garnished with garlic butter, as a magnificent ally of the great Touraine roasts. Inevitably, too, the rivers around Tours furnish the basis of excellent dishes: fresh salmon from January to July; pike; carp, again often cooked in Vouvray.

After such a meal I can think of no better treat than an evening walk away from the church of Saint-Julien and east along the river bank as far as the Château-Royal, whose medieval Tour Guise is often subtly illuminated and whose renaissance governor's house is at all times romantic and at night quite magical. Its name really ought to annoy the British, since it derives from the imprisonment of the Duc de Guise here between 1588 and 1591, whereas the building was paid for by the English King Henry II. Château-Royal has been turned into a museum, with tableaux illustrating the whole history of the Loire valley. The quai d'Orléans, which it overlooks, leads past the narrow, easily missed place Foire-le-Roi which contains the lovely Hôtel Babou de la Bourdaisière, built in 1520 by the finance minister of King François I.

The fifteenth-century quarters of Tours unexpectedly reveal delightfully carved half-timbered houses.

89

In spite of the depredations of war, Tours has clearly not lost all of its past. Tours is a city to explore by walking, not by car. Here are two of my favourite walks. The first starts at the railway station and ends at the wine museum next to the church of Saint-Julien. The prefecture, close by the railway station, is housed in a former eighteenth-century convent of the Visitation. The city boasts a pleasing number of old hôtels (the word in this context means of course 'mansions' and not 'hotels'), and this walk takes you past two historically fascinating ones. You reach the first, Hôtel Mame, by walking north from the prefecture along rue Corneille and turning left into rue Émile Zola. Hôtel Mame is an elegant eighteenth-century mansion in the style known as Louis XV. Once the home of a prosperous Nantes ship-owner (Lefebre de Montifray), it illustrates its own glorious past with a splendid wrought-iron gateway on which sails the ship of fortune. Inside is a magnificent staircase, decorated with bronze wild animals set at bay by the dogs of huntsmen, as well as rooms displaying Gobelin tapestries. The publisher Arnold Mame restored this hôtel in 1913, adding a lavish rotunda and rich galleries.

Continue north from rue Émile Zola along rue de Lucé and across rue de la Scellerie to the garden and fountain (dated 1510) of Beaune-Semblançay, in rue J. Favre. Jacques de Beaune-Semblançay lived here in the early sixteenth century in the partially surviving renaissance hôtel that bears his name. He was hanged at Montfaucon in 1527. A few paces north of the garden and you are back at the church and wine museum of Saint-Julien.

The second walk takes you from here through the sixteenth century to the Middle Ages, by way of a series of domestic architectural treats. Happily the early sixteenth-century renaissance facade of Hôtel Gouin (No. 25 rue du Commerce, which is a continuation west of rue Colbert from the church of Saint-Julien) was not destroyed in a disastrous fire of June 1940. A fine staircase-tower to the north also survived. Here is Tours in its Italian aspect, the taste of a merchant named René Gardette who owned Hôtel Gouin in the early sixteenth century. Everything has been praiseworthily restored. Somehow the one brick chimney seems to humanize the whole sumptuous hôtel. Even if the archaeological museum that it now houses is not to your liking, to walk through Hôtel Gouin is still a rare treat.

My favourite street in Tours is rue Paul-Louis-Courier, running northwest from rue du Commerce, delightfully unexpected, almost totally unspoiled. It is hard to set a date to all the houses in rue Paul-Louis-Courier, but No. 7 comprises two sixteenth-century dwellings. No. 9 dates from the seventeenth century (do not miss the wooden staircase inside its courtyard),

The splendid renaissance entrance of the Hôtel Gouin, Tours.

No. 15 (Hôtel Robin-Quentin) is again sixteenth century and No. 17 (Hôtel Juste) was built even earlier.

Follow the streets west here, guessing at the dates of buildings or simply enjoying their charm, as far as place Plumereau, the centre of medieval Tours and meticulously restored. Here some of the buildings are even more ancient than those in the surrounding streets: at No. 7 a courtyard leads you to the remains of a romanesque church built in the twelfth century; at the corner of rue de Change is a lovely fifteenth-century building roofed in grey slates; and the whole south side of the square is made up of picturesque gabled houses. Rue Briçonnet, leading out of place Plumereau, boasts among other treasures a thirteenth-century house with a romanesque facade, and at No. 16 the splendid, beautifully-restored, late fifteenth-century Hôtel Pierre-du-Puy.

Tours today reveals little of its Gallo-Roman past, but just outside the city is a charming survival from this era. Drive west along the right bank of the Loire (the road is the N152) to the village of Luynes. Long before the village existed this was the site of a Gallo-Roman villa. Paul-Louis Courier, who gave his name to my favourite street in Tours, lived at Luynes in the early nineteenth century. He was a writer and vintner more noted now for the fact that his young, bored wife bestowed so many favours on other men that when he finally put a stop to this, one of them almost certainly shot him dead. Opposite the church in the village is another rue Paul-Louis-Courier. On its corner is a fifteenth-century half-timbered house carved with figures of St Matthew, St Christopher and a Piéta – but who is the third saint? Drive up this street and first left along rue de l'Alma into the cemetery for a splendid view of the late medieval château, glaring balefully down on the dead, its grey stone walls and four towers relieved by not a single machicolation.

Luynes is lovely: some troglodyte dwellings in the hillsides, an old mill, two more châteaux (both built in the nineteenth century). Drive back to the corner of rue Paul-Louis-Courier and across the road, to the street that winds upwards past the fifteenth-century wooden market hall (a very steep roof), still in use. You drive on past houses dated 1655 to the top of the plateau that fringes the Loire here, as far as the utterly charming Gallo-Roman aqueduct – at least 1500 years old and standing perilously above the village. Tall stone pillars and arches, strengthened by red tiles, flank the roadside. I should not be able to go to sleep at night in the houses that nestle under some of the leaning piers.

Drive a further 9 kilometres along the N152, with cherry trees flanking the wide river, to Cinq-Mars-la-Pile to see, by contrast with the aqueduct of Luynes, an extraordinarily ugly Gallo-Roman monument, a sort of red chimney sparsely decorated with white tiles. Standing above the village are a couple of far more attractive towers, ruins of the feudal château. The château is a ruin because in 1642 Cardinal Richelieu ordered its destruction after executing the Marquis of Cinq-Mars for plotting against him. (These aristocratic feuds inspired Alfred de Vigny's romantic novel *Cinq Mars*, published in 1826. In Vigny's account the young marquis and his faithful friend Thou, let down by their allies, go uncomplainingly and courageously to their deaths.) As for the bizarre name of this village, its derivation is curious. First known as the land of St Médard, it gradually evolved into Saint-Mars and then (by the sixteenth century) into Cinq-Mars.

Whereas the ruined château of Cinq-Mars-la-Pile seems oddly remote from the village, the château at Langeais, further along the N152, is very much part of the town. Foulques Nerra built a keep here at the end of the tenth century and much more was built over the next 300 years. Then the English took the château and razed it. Jean Bourré, treasurer to Louis XI, rebuilt the château in the mid fifteenth century just in time to celebrate the marriage of Charles VIII and Anne of Brittany here in 1491. Since the marriage marked the reunion of Brittany and France, the young bride (aged

Left The uncompromisingly military face which the old château at Luynes presents to the world conceals a charming early renaissance home inside the walls.

Below The superb sixteenth-century gardens at Villandry, southwest of Luynes, fell into disrepair until they were lovingly restored in the early twentieth century.

Left When Jean le Breton, secretary of state to King François I, bought the ancient château of Villandry in 1532, he transformed every part, save the old square keep, into a château as fine as those of his royal master.

Above The château at Langeais, rebuilt in the mid fifteenth century, where Charles VIII and Anne of Brittany were married in 1491. Even today, in spite of several restorations, the château presents a formidable front to the world.

95

scarcely fifteen) was pledged in the event of Charles's untimely death to marry his successor. One delicate feature of this powerful building is its drawbridge, in two parts, the smaller, narrower one wide enough to admit only pedestrians. The interior is much less forbidding than the outside, and is splendidly furnished.

As you leave the château you notice the corner house opposite, classical in design, with fluted shallow columns, declaring itself to be the house of François Rabelais, though there is little enough evidence that the great humanist writer ever lived here. The facade alone is classical. Inside the house a twisting medieval staircase leads up to the first floor.

You can walk across the river with its attractive weirs on the old bridge to see a piece of architectural vandalism: the church of Saint-Jean-Baptiste. Until 1869 this was a romanesque basilica dating from the eleventh and twelfth centuries. Then the whole was savagely restored, and a couple of transepts, with two rose windows, were added. The work is well done and colourfully decorated inside and out. But one cannot help wishing it could be undone. The old belfry is lovely, with a staircase-tower that begins square and becomes round half-way up. The entrance still has its fifteenth-century vaulting. The simple, tiny crypt (entered by a gate on the left-hand side of the high altar) may date even from as early as the tenth century. Do not miss the eleventh-century carvings on the outside of the apse.

You drive across the river at Langeais by the impressive suspension bridge. In 10 kilometres you reach what the people of Indre-et-Loire describe as the most feminine of all the châteaux of the Loire valley, Azay-le-Rideau, 'a many-faceted diamond set in the River Indre', as Balzac described it. This French/Italian renaissance château was largely built by Gilles Berthelot, a wealthy citizen of Tours who was forced to flee for his life in 1527 for complicity with the misdemeanours of the hanged Jacques de Beaune-Semblançay. The not quite finished Azay-le-Rideau was given by King François I to a favourite named Antoine Raffin. In the early nineteenth century the state paid 200,000 francs for the château.

The château appears today substantially as it was built (save for some reordering of its lake). The new renaissance style, inspired partly by French military adventures in Italy (seen here above all in the great monumental staircase), has not totally overwhelmed the allure of gothic at Azay-le-Rideau. And it is still ironic to discover that Gilles Berthelot, before his disgrace, had François I's device of a salamander carved sycophantically on the building. The interior of Azay-le-Rideau has been fittingly set out as a museum of the renaissance, with excellent tapestries and furniture, and splendid bedrooms.

The countryside is now more interesting, with copses of all sizes, hillocks and many great trees. Cross the Indre at Azay-le-Rideau and turn east along the D17 to Saché. Balzac was a frequent guest of M. and Mme de Margonne, who owned the château here and had been great friends of his parents (M. de Margonne particularly friendly, people said, with Balzac's mother). The novelist needed the solitude of his own sparse room here. 'I kiss the view of the Indre and the little château, which I call Clochegourde,' he wrote in *Le Lys dans la vallée* (*The Lily of the Valley*), which is set here. 'The silence is marvellous.' He also frequently needed money. In 1834 he told his future wife (Countess Hanska), 'I leave for Saché on the 20th. There, in the calm and quiet, I must produce two octavo volumes, for the money problem is frightful.' At Saché he would rise at 2 am and write and write, fortified by coffee and toast. Here he produced some of

---

Technically-speaking, Azay-le-Rideau is a gothic château, yet its spirit is that of the Italian renaissance which was seeping into France in the early sixteenth century.

Left The church of Saint-Maurice, built 1527, restored 1867, in the pretty village of Crissay-sur-Manse south of Azay-le-Rideau.

Below The entrancing château at Ussé on the bank of the River Indre inspired Charles Perrault's fairy tale *The Sleeping Beauty*.

his greatest works: *Les Illusions perdues* (*Lost Illusions*), and *César Birotteau* as well as *Le Lys dans la vallée*. Here he worked out the themes of *Le Père Goriot*. Often he would appear in the village acting out various characters before his friends, and – since little seems to have changed here – it is pleasant to sit in the twelfth-century inn at Saché and muse that he might still appear and do so. He thought the women of Saché had the most beautiful shoulders he had ever seen.

The château is basically a large sixteenth- and seventeenth-century manor house. You can visit its drawing room, perfectly furnished in the style of Louis-Philippe, where Balzac's hosts would give parties for the writer (till at ten o'clock he would feel the need to go to bed for his four hours of sleep). The first floor has portraits of Balzac, his family and his acquaintances. Next door is his bedroom, kept as it was when he sat writing either in his curtained bed or in front of the window at the small desk, by the light of a single candle. In other rooms are statues of characters from his *Comédie Humaine*, caricatures of himself and his contemporaries, first editions of his works and corrected manuscripts. The windows look out onto the solitary countryside and great oak trees he described in *Le Lys dans la vallée*, 'too grave for superficial folk, dear to the tender souls of poets'.

The heroine of *Le Lys dans la vallée* is buried in the church at Saché. Saint-Martin-de-Vertou stands today exactly as Balzac knew it, a nave with Angevin vaulting, a three-cornered apse, a square thirteenth-century tower, stalls with carved misericords and a fine seventeenth-century altar.

Just beyond Saché take the D19 southeast through Thilouze (where they still show you the house of Balzac's gardener) on to Villeperdue. Here is a pretty renaissance château, restored in the nineteenth century and far less threatening than most. A child could swim across its moat. Drive on across the motorway, turn right along the N10 and look out for the sign left to Sainte-Catherine-de-Fierbois.

Although most tourists speed their way along the N10 heedless of this little town, Sainte-Catherine-de-Fierbois has played a central part in the history of France. Its name derives from a bone of St Catherine of Alexandria which the Maréchal de Boucicaut brought here from Mount Sinai in the Middle Ages. ('Fierbois' simply means 'savage forest'.) The relic attracted pilgrims en route from Paris through Tours to Santiago de Compostela, hence the almonry and hospice built here for them by Boucicaut in 1415. The restored almonry today doubles up as the town hall and presbytery of Sainte-Catherine-de-Fierbois.

Inside the church is a lovely fifteenth-century statue of the saint, with the Catherine-wheel on which she

St Catherine of Alexandria, with the wheel on which she was broken: a statue in the church at Sainte-Catherine-de-Fierbois, where a relic of the saint apparently spoke to Joan of Arc on 5 March 1429.

was broken and martyred. The old chapel of St Catherine was destroyed by a fire around 1440. Fifty years later it was replaced by another in the flamboyant gothic style. On the altar is sculpted St Catherine, between the arms of Charles VIII and Anne of Brittany. Their arms are on the roof-bosses too, and this chapel houses a superbly carved confessional.

One saint inspires another. On 5 March 1429 Joan of Arc stayed here on her way to Chinon from Loches. She prayed before the relic and statue of St Catherine and heard the saint reply. Now the sword with which Charles Martel had repulsed the Saracens in the year 732 was thought to have been left here. The sword had long since disappeared. Joan of Arc left the town in 1429, and three days later sent back a messenger to find this very sword behind the altar of St Catherine, with five crosses marked on its blade.

The church at Sainte-Catherine-de-Fierbois is basically Angevin gothic in style. Its main doorway – one of the finest flamboyant porches in Touraine – is matched in miniature by the charming entrance to the nearby 'Maison du Dauphin', built in 1415. Look for the fifteenth-century carving depicting the entombment of Jesus on the north wall of the church. Outside in the main square of Sainte-Catherine-de-Fierbois stands a nineteenth-century statue of St Joan of Arc.

Directly west of Sainte-Catherine-de-Fierbois, over the N10 and the motorway and along the D21, lies Avon-les-Roches, reached by way of the picturesque little village of Crissay-sur-Manse. (Much care has gone into restoring Crissay-sur-Manse, with its old houses and fine flamboyant church.) The church of Notre-Dame at Avon-les-Roches has an extraordinarily beautiful romanesque porch – protected by an equally remarkable eleventh-century roofed lean-to. There is next-to-nothing else here, and you have to get the key to the church at the grocery (épicerie) opposite. The shopkeeper is happy to show people round, and was one day about to lock the church (lamenting its dankness) when I suggested that other tourists might like to see it without always troubling her. (Notre-Dame at Avon-les-Roches possesses, for instance, not one but two romanesque fonts. In addition, it does an old building good to be aired.) She promised to leave the church open, at least *for the rest of that afternoon.* I went for refreshment to the gloomy bar in the square just round the corner.

Drive on a little way and then take the D757 south to the ship-like island in the middle of the River Vienne, an island lying at the heart of L'Île-Bouchard. This town dates from the fortress which a certain Bouchard founded here about 880. The rest of the town is divided between each bank of the river, each half with its own church, the south bank also boasting the remains of the romanesque priory of Saint-Léonard. The capitals of its columns are fantastic. (You get inside by asking for the key at the farm next door.) The château at L'Île-Bouchard is modest, save for an extremely pretentious gateway.

Three kilometres away along the D760 is Tavant. Even if you think you have seen enough churches for one day, find the lady who looks after the church of Saint-Nicolas here and pay to see the beautiful twelfth-century frescoes in the crypt. Huge round columns divide this crypt into three, and the scenes painted on the walls reveal many of the themes that peopled the minds of eleventh-century Christians. Two men hold beams to build the Jerusalem Temple. King David plays his lyre, dances and fights a lion. Adam delves and Eve spins. St Peter is crucified upside-down. Jesus visits souls in Purgatory and is also pictured in his glory. The faces and the folds of the garments are Byzantine. The colours are blue, yellow-ochre, green, red, black and white. One or two frescoes are unfinished, sketched out but uncoloured. A few are difficult to decipher. Who is the pilgrim to the right of the entrance? He wears sandals and carries a palm and staff, but he does not sport the cockleshell of St James.

A fresco of the Virgin Mary is painted opposite the symbol of lust. But lust has become the most celebrated

Left **The crumbling, exquisite romanesque church doorways at Avon-les-Roches.**

Above **The fifteenth-century château of Le Rivau, north of Richelieu, is as sumptuous inside as it is outside.**

103

fresco at Tavant: a beautiful woman bleeding profusely, her breast pierced by a lance.

Frescoes also decorate the nave of Tavant church. The early twelfth-century painting of Christ in Majesty, in a radiant circle of light containing the four evangelists and four angels, was uncovered only in 1945. On the south side of the apse are depicted the annunciation, visitation and nativity. On the north side are fragments of angels and of the flight into Egypt. Not to be outdone, the carved romanesque capitals display a rare fierceness. Here are wild beasts, scenes of temptation, two sirens, and a monster eating a naked man.

The D757 now leads southwest to Richelieu, but make a rewarding detour west at La Simardière to Champigny-sur-Veude (or go directly across country from Tavant). Here what seems to be an unusual château set athwart the road actually consists of no more than the remarkable outbuildings left when Cardinal Richelieu bought and destroyed the great family home of the Bourbon, Montpensier, in the seventeenth century. The cardinal was determined that nothing in the neighbourhood should overtop the new town he had just built and named after himself. Fortunately he acceded to the Pope's request not to demolish the chapel, which Louis I de Bourbon had built in the early sixteenth century in memory of his saintly predecessor Louis IX.

Everything here is gleaming white, rising from long green lawns, set amidst formal gardens and court-yards. A chunky dormer sits at either end of the outbuildings. A covered cloister leads from them to the chapel. The countless 'Ls' sculpted on the exterior of the chapel and carved on its ornate doorway make one ask who really owned God's house. Inside, a side-chapel was built to house the black marble tomb of Henri de Bourbon, Duke of Montpensier. His praying effigy has been removed from the top of this tomb and given greater glory in the very middle of the main chapel.

The real glory of the chapel at Champigny-sur-Veude is the sublime colours of its renaissance windows, given by Cardinal Claude de Givry, Bishop of Langres. Again, however, one asks who is being honoured. True, there are scenes from the life of Jesus here, including a luminous crucifixion. And here is Saint Louis in Reims Cathedral. But here too crowd in far lesser kings and nobles of France.

La Fontaine described the town of Richelieu, 6 kilometres due south of Champigny-sur-Veude, as 'the

---

Right **A jewel of the renaissance: the gleaming Sainte-Chapelle at Champigny-sur-Veude, built by Louis I de Bourbon in the first half of the sixteenth century.**

Below **One of the classical gateways designed by Jacques Lemercier for Cardinal Richelieu's new town, named after himself, built in the early seventeenth century.**

most beautiful village in the universe'. Some say he spoke ironically, but Richelieu is certainly a fascinating piece of aristocratic town planning. Cardinal Richelieu rebuilt it like a classical French *bastide* – that is, in the form of a fortified rectangle. Impressive classical gateways, a classical church, regular noble homes, long straight streets at right-angles to each other, a market place and a square at either end of the town were created by the architects Jacques Lemercier (famous for part of the Louvre and the Sorbonne) and his brother Pierre. Where Richelieu differs from a medieval *bastide* (in which there was no feudal lord and the citizens shared equal rights) is that the cardinal also commissioned Jacques, Pierre and their brother Nicolas Lemercier to build him a great ducal château in a monumental park that embraces 475 hectares of land. The château remained in the hands of the cardinal's heirs until the Revolution. It was almost entirely demolished in 1805, as an unwelcome symbol of the old régime. Happily the statue of the cardinal, brought here from Versailles in 1932, stands outside the gates of the park as a reminder of the great prince of the Church and ruthless courtier who refounded the town in the seventeenth century.

Loudun, 16 kilometres west of Richelieu by an absolutely straight road, could not present a greater contrast. Its battered and broken keep and château dominate narrow twisting streets. The old church of Sainte-Croix (with an eleventh-century choir) is now filled with market stalls. Théophraste Renaudot, who published the first newspaper printed in France (*La Gazette de France*), was born here in 1585, close by the renaissance church of Saint-Pierre. In his day Loudun was a haven for protestants, who were implacably hated by Cardinal Richelieu and driven out after the Revocation of the Edict of Nantes in 1685, an event greatly contributing to Loudun's decline.

Foulques Nerra built the old square keep of the town, and some of his savagery seems to have lingered on here. In 1634 a twenty-seven-year-old priest named Urbain Grandier was accused of subjecting local Ursuline nuns to demoniac possession. He was found guilty and publicly burnt to death in place Sainte-Croix. Aldous Huxley (in *The Devils of Loudun*) recalled the savage zeal of Grandier's enemies. 'They sprinkled the wood, the straw, the glowing coals of the brazier that stood ready beside the pyre; they sprinkled the earth, the air, the victim, the executioners, the spectators. This time, they swore, no devil should prevent the wretch from suffering to the extreme limit of his capacity for pain.'

Chinon, lying on the Vienne some 50 kilometres northeast of Loudun, justly deserves its reputation as a tourist attraction, even though the town in consequence can become almost unbearably full. At such times one can pleasingly escape during the tourist season by taking an excursion on a train drawn by a 1920s steam locomotive through Champigny-sur-Veude as far as Richelieu and back.

The road from Loudun meets the D751 where you turn right before taking a left turn across the river into Chinon. The curtain wall of the château (really three châteaux in one), high up above the rooftops, runs almost the whole length of the town, which is hemmed in by the river into a long, lovely narrow strip. Although purists have criticised some of the restoration of this enchanting place, it is still possible to imagine yourself back eight centuries in time, when Henry II of England died here. In 1199 his son, Richard the Lionheart, came mortally wounded to die at Chinon. Three hundred and forty years later Joan of Arc met the dauphin here. The dauphin tried to hide from the saint amongst his retainers, but she instantly recognized him, though

The long wall of Chinon château overlooks both the little town and the River Vienne. Note the octagonal spire of the church of Saint-Maurice, added in the fifteenth century and decorated with Limoges enamel.

they had never met, and announced her divine mission to save both him and his realm.

François Rabelais' father Antoine was a Chinon lawyer and his son was born nearby at the end of the fifteenth century. Since Rabelais' famous character Gargantua came into the world demanding drink, the great novelist has been made patron saint of Chinon wine and the brethren of the 'Entonneurs Rabelaisiens de Chinon' regularly dress in their red, gold and blue robes and meet at his birthplace (now a Rabelais museum), situated at La Devinière (7½ kilometres southwest of the town), to sing the praises of their great vintages. Ruby in colour, fragrant as violets, Chinon, they insist, is the one wine for the connoisseur. Rabelais would have agreed.

The D751 leads directly back from Chinon to Tours, but if you have time take a small detour right at Azay-le-Rideau by way of Montbazon, to see the massive ruined keep built by Foulques Nerra and since 1866 bizarrely topped by an enormous copper Virgin Mary.

From Tours drive east along the south bank of the Loire to Amboise. In 1882 Henry James described the same Amboise as we see today: 'A little white-faced town, staring across an admirable bridge, and leaning, behind, as it were, against the pedestal of rock on which the dark castle masses itself.' He added, 'The town is so small, the pedestal so big, and the castle so high and striking, that the clustered houses at the base of the rock are like the crumbs that have fallen from a well-laden table.'

Amboise is today so gentle that it is scarcely possible to believe that Huguenots plotted here in 1560 to kidnap King François II (husband of Mary Stuart). They were discovered and beheaded or gruesomely

---

Hidden among the trees amid lush fields is a manor house at Saint-Germain-sur-Vienne, near Chinon.

hanged from the walls of Henry James' striking castle. In contemporary prints of the massacre, the slaughtered Huguenots at first appear to be devoutly praying until you realize that their hands have been tightly bound together. A more charming memory is the welcome given by François I to Leonardo da Vinci, who lived until his death in 1519 at the second château at Amboise, Château Clos-Lucé (600 metres from the city centre along rue Victor-Hugo). The IBM company has recreated some of his remarkable inventions in the Leonardo museum here, works of scientific genius thought out long before their time had come.

Both châteaux at Amboise are well worth exploring. You reach the main one by way of rue François-Ier, between the town hall and the church of Saint-Florent (the town hall built in 1505, the church, apart from its renaissance bell-tower, between 1447 and 1484). This château is nothing like its medieval and renaissance self, having been partially demolished under Napoleon and used as a public gaol. It is still lovely in an evening light, overlooking the graceful bridge that spans the river far below. Its gothic chapel dedicated to St Hubert (who discovered a crucifix in the antlers of a hunted stag) bristles with antlers.

For the energetic, a little excursion south of the river reaches (within 3 kilometres along the D31) the lovely 'Chinese' pagoda of Chanteloup, erected in 1762, where you can climb 149 steps for a view as far as Tours to the west and Blois to the northeast over the forest of Amboise (which covers 5000 hectares). And from the pagoda the same road runs south as far as the River Cher, where you turn left to visit the gorgeous château of Chenonceaux. This is one of the masterpieces of the whole Loire valley. The deputy treasurer of Normandy, Thomas Bohier, had begun building the château on the site of an old manor house, which he bought in 1513. Ten years later he died, but his widow carried on the work, only to find that the château had to be sold to the king to pay her husband's death duties. The initials TBK (why K?) on the building

Left Amboise, where the Loire joins the River Amasse, with its splendid château, half sombre, half outrageously flamboyant.

Below Chenonceaux, with the arched bridge of Diane de Poitiers on which Catherine de Medici constructed a superb gallery: two royal ladies at odds, together creating a masterpiece.

overlooking the terrace are a memento of Thomas Bohier and his wife Catherine Briçonnet.

The next king, Henri II, gave Chenonceaux to his mistress Diane de Poitiers, and she it was who first employed the architect Philippe Delorme to create the gardens and throw the stupendous bridge across the River Cher. As soon as Henri II died, his widow Catherine de Medici forced Diane to give her the château. Happily Catherine continued to employ Delorme in adding the long gallery over the bridge, in

building magnificent stables and in laying out the park. Inside, the sumptuous rooms are in exquisite condition, decorated for the most part in the style of the next century, but retaining such renaissance features as Diane de Poitier's superb chimney (embellished with her initials enlacing Henri's).

It is fascinating to compare such elegant châteaux as Chenonceaux with the fearsome defensive châteaux of earlier ages, such as the one at Montrichard 9 kilometres east along the Cher, where the walls of the enormous ruined keep are no less than 3 metres thick at the base.

From Montrichard drive along the D764 to Loches. En route, walled and aloof in a field at Montpoupon, stands another sort of château, quite strange, turreted and with brick chimneys. Inside it looks like a rather large farmhouse, which is precisely what it is. Then you pass through Genillé, where the twelfth-century church of Sainte-Eulalie seems to fill the entire place Agnès-Sorel. It houses many treasures. Inside, its roof is a beautiful barrel-vault, with colourfully painted diaper work and decorated tie beams. The apse is early gothic, boasting a fine traceried east window, and here the lierne vaulting has twisted to the left over the centuries. The vessel for holy water is dated 1494 and is inscribed, *'Qui a donné ce bénitier en Paradis à son chantier'* ('The one who gave this font has his building-site in Paradise'). As if these treasures were not enough, Sainte-Eulalie at Genillé has a renaissance gallery and a seventeenth-century pulpit decorated with gilded evangelists and the sacred heart of Jesus.

Genillé is well-blessed with châteaux. My favourite is Château de Marolles, built between the fifteenth and seventeenth centuries and restored in the nineteenth. You find it by walking up rue Adam-Fumée.

Left **Montpoupon is half a château and half a fortified farmhouse, seen here from its ancient pigeon-house.**

Finally you reach Loches. The writer Alfred de Vigny was born here and, I think, underestimated the town of his birth, observing, 'people say it is pretty'. Loches is an extraordinarily pretty town. Like many another in the Loire valley, its main street seems dominated by the château until the spires of the church of Saint-Ours come into view. The town grew around a fifth-century monastery dedicated to St Ursus, of Cahors, but curiously enough this is not the true successor of the monastery church. That was destroyed at the Revolution, so the citizens of Loches blithely renamed the church of Notre-Dame as Saint-Ours (forgetting that Notre-Dame had been built to house one of Our Lady's girdles). St Ours was fortunate in his new church. Its four splendid spires were built in the mid twelfth century. The main doorway is

Far from fearsome lions and medieval beasts guard the château at Loches.

Above Between Montrésor and Loches lies the
Charterhouse of Liget, which the English King
Henry II founded to expiate the murder of
Archbishop Thomas Becket.

Right The fierceness of the past: the remains of
the formidable keep at Le Grand-Pressigny
south of Loches.

magically sculpted with monkeys, monsters and other beasts. Another entrancingly paradoxical feature of the church of Saint-Ours is its font, made out of a Gallo-Roman altar once used for pagan sacrifices.

Loches boasts extremely impressive renaissance gateways: porte Royale, porte des Cordeliers, and porte Picois in place Hôtel de Ville. You can still see the grooves of the portcullis of porte Picois. In a niche over the gate is a statue of the Virgin Mary giving her child an apple. Abutting this gate is the superb sixteenth-century town hall of Loches. Here are houses from the same era, with fine twisting staircases. More sinister are the notorious dungeons of Le Martelet, where desperate prisoners have carved graffiti (one of the most desperate being Ludovico Sforza, who was so evilly treated during the eight years of his imprisonment, which began in 1500, that he failed to recover after his release).

The medieval château is surrounded by 3 kilometres of ramparts, within which a completely separate part of the town grew up. Inside these ramparts stands the building that gives Loches its most romantic frisson: the Logis du Roi. Charles VIII and Anne of Brittany lived here, a spiral staircase climbing up to her tiny oratory, with its delicate arches, its fine cable-moulding and its sculpted ermine. And here is the tomb of Agnès Sorel.

The most celebrated portrait of this beautiful young Touraine woman shows her with her left hand delicately marking the pages of a book, her eyes downcast, her shoulders lightly veiled and her left breast bared. At the age of twenty she entranced Charles VII and became his mistress. In spite of her many charities, her enemies fulminated against her luxuries and immorality. This was the first time that a king of France had openly acknowledged a mistress.

The River Creuse flows languidly near the village of Barrou south of Loches.

Charles gave her land and châteaux. And she undoubtedly rescued the king from his dangerous indolence. The great historian Jules Michelet went so far as to attribute to her France's salvation. She bore Charles three daughters, and died pregnant by him a fourth time at Jumièges in 1450, on her way to join the king as he was finally driving the English out of France.

Her heart and entrails were buried at Jumièges. The rest of Agnès Sorel's body was brought back to Loches, which she had chosen as her home, and placed in a black marble tomb in the monastery church of which she had been so great a benefactress. A white marble effigy of the royal mistress was sculpted to lie on this tomb. Not long afterwards Charles VII was solacing himself in the arms of her niece.

At the Revolution the tomb of Agnès Sorel was thrown out of the church at Loches and savagely hacked to pieces (possibly because some impious revolutionaries mistakenly took it as the effigy of a saint). Her corpse was burned and mocked, but in 1809 the ashes were put back in her meticulously restored tomb. This was now placed, not in the church at Loches, but in a tower of the château. You cannot tell from the face how beautiful she was, since this is a totally imaginative portrait.

From Loches a short drive northwest along the N143 leads directly back to Tours. On the way you pass the ancient village of Dolus-le-Sec a short distance west of the main road (with its eleventh-century church and eighteenth-century Château de l'Épinay). Half-way between Dolus-le-Sec and Tours is the fascinating town of Cormery. The abbot of Saint-Martin of Tours founded an abbey here in 791, and much remains of its fourteenth- and fifteenth-century buildings, as well as a circular defensive tower that protected the whole town. The church of Notre-Dame at Cormery was built in the twelfth century, and if you have time, go inside to enjoy its frescoes, statues and the grotesque faces carved on its twelfth-century font.

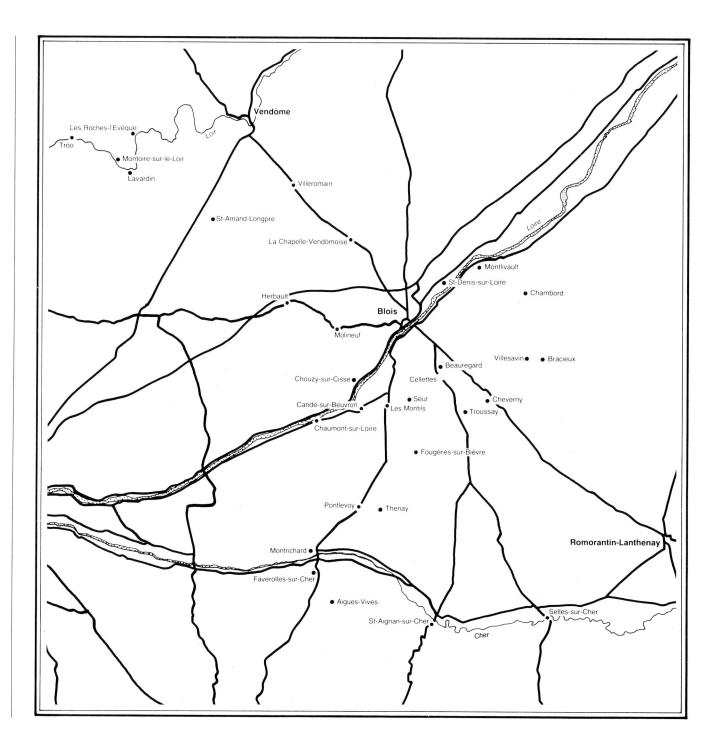

Vendôme

Les Roches-l'Evèque

Tróo

Montoire-sur-le-Loir

Lavardin

Loir

Villeromain

St-Amand-Longpre

La Chapelle-Vendômoise

Montlivault

St-Denis-sur-Loire

Chambord

Loire

Herbault

Blois

Molineuf

Villesavin ● ● Bracieux

Beauregard

Chouzy-sur-Cisse

Cellettes

Seur

Cande-sur-Beuvron ● Les Montils

Cheverny

Troussay

Chaumont-sur-Loire

Fougères-sur-Bièvre

Pontlevoy ● Thenay

Romorantin-Lanthenay

Montrichard ●

Faverolles-sur-Cher

Aigues-Vives

Selles-sur-Cher

St-Aignan-sur-Cher

Cher

4
Cave-dwellings and Châteaux

Blois – Chaumont-sur-Loire – Chambord –
Cheverny – Montrichard – Romorantin-Lanthenay
– Trôo – Vendôme

On Thursday 22 December 1588 the Duke of Guise, leader of the Catholic League in the Wars of Religion, sat down to dine in the château at Blois, which was then the seat of the King of France. He was handed a napkin concealing a note of warning: 'Take care, someone is about to do you harm.' Guise read the note, wrote on it, 'No one would dare,' and threw it under the table.

Henri of Lorraine, Duke of Guise and cousin of the king, had many enemies. At the meeting of the Estates General of 1476 the catholics led by the Guise family had managed to annul a series of concessions to French protestants. The duke had taken a leading role in the notorious massacre of St Bartholomew's Day. He had foiled the attempted truce in the Wars of Religion planned by King Henri III and the protestant Henri of Navarre. By 1588 the king had further cause to hate the duke, for Guise was extremely popular in Paris and the Parisians had turned against the monarchy. Henri III called the Estates General to Blois determined to deal with his overmighty subject. The day after Guise had contemptuously ignored the warning in the napkin, some of the king's gentlemen-in-waiting seized him by the arms and stabbed him in the chest. The dying duke managed to drag his assassins from one end of the room

to the other, as far as the foot of the king's bed, before expiring with the prayer, 'Be merciful to me, O God.' The king entered the room, gazed at the dead man, and made the celebrated remark, 'He looks even bigger dead than alive!' Guise's friends were seized and subsequently massacred. And the following day, Christmas Eve, one of Henri III's allies confronted the dead man's brother, the Cardinal of Lorraine, in Blois prison with the words 'Monsieur, think of God,' before plunging a fatal dagger into his back.

By his complicity in these murders King Henri III had signed his own death warrant. On 1 April 1589 he himself was assassinated. But in the meantime he and Henri of Navarre had entered into the alliance which helped to bring the latter to the throne of France and, within four years, to his own assassination. Small wonder if the court at this point decided to abandon Blois for Paris.

In the château at Blois you are still shown Henri III's apartments, where the murder of the Duke of Guise took place. You reach them by the 'staircase of the forty-five', so-called not because of the number of its steps but because the king had forty-five gentlemen-in-waiting. In the council chamber are two splendid fireplaces; in front of one Guise is said to have been warming himself just before his assassination. The great council chamber at Blois has scarcely changed since 143 clergy, 180 nobility and 191 representatives of the Third Estate assembled here in 1588 for the fateful meeting of the Estates General. The build-up to the assassination was both lavish and tense. Guise, dressed in silk, had appeared insolent to his royal cousin. The queen-mother, Catherine de Medici, close to the end of her life (she died nine days after Christmas), had given a sumptuous ball. Henri III had condemned those who were forming alliances destined to divide his kingdom in order – he alleged – to further their own ambitions. Until the duke's murder, few would have believed Henri capable of changing the situation. The room in which he plotted the murder is today largely as it was restored in the nineteenth century, but you are still shown the door behind which the king is said to have hidden while his cousin's assassination took place.

The château at Blois is filled with such melodramatic associations. Another room, on the first floor of the same wing, is dubbed the 'cabinet of poisons' (or else the 'cabinet of Catherine de Medici'). It boasts 230 carved panels, of which four open (by a secret device) to reveal little hidden cupboards designed to contain whatever nefarious substances the owner might like to keep there. (Truth to tell, alas for the melodramatic school of history, such secret cabinets were a harmless craze of many sixteenth-century great houses.)

The château of Blois is also varied and beautiful. Its staircases alone are entrancing. That of the forty-five is a spiral renaissance masterpiece, richly decorated with Corinthian capitals, and with salamanders over the doorways. In the middle of this wing is an open staircase tower of 1520, octagonal and magical (the work of the architect Jacques Sourdeau), the steps inside curving elegantly round a central pillar. To the northeast of this side of the château, a couple of staircase-towers flank the Italianate Louis XII wing built between 1498 and 1503. Opposite, the wing built by François Mansart in the early seventeenth century boasts a majestic classical stairway.

Yet the château began modestly enough. The remarkable poet Charles d'Orléans – a member of the French royal family whose own father had been assassinated; a husband who married at fifteen and lost his first young wife in 1409, only to lose a second six years later; a soldier who spent twenty-five years in the tower of London, taken prisoner by the English at the battle of Agincourt – made a home for his fellow artists here, in a simple fourteenth-century château.

At Blois he organized poetry competitions in which his great contemporary François Villon took part. One theme, upon which Villon's verses proved victorious, was 'I am dying of thirst beside a fountain'. You can see why Villon won. He transformed the theme into a terrifying meditation on the impossibility of achieving happiness:

'I am dying of thirst beside a fountain,
Hot as fire, yet trembling in every tooth;
In my own land I seem far away;
Close by the fire and all aflame, I freeze;
Naked as a worm, I dress in furs;
I laugh through my tears, waiting hopelessly,
My only comfort sorrowful despair,
Rejoicing, I take no pleasure;
Strong, I have no force or power;
Welcomed, I am rebuffed by all.

The one sure fact is the uncertainty of everything,
And what is obvious proves obscure;
The moment I am confident, I fall into doubts;
Knowledge springs from happenstance. . . .'

Villon had arrived at Blois in 1487, a fugitive charged with the murder of a priest. Charles d'Orléans was his

---

The magical staircase tower of the château at Blois.

The salamander, symbol of King François I, carved on the château at Blois.

senior by thirty-seven years but the two men became fast friends.

Charles d'Orléans' third wife bore him two daughters and a son, Louis. The French court at this time resided at Amboise. In 1498 King Charles VIII, returning from a tennis match, hit his head against a lintel and unexpectedly died. Louis became King Louis XII of France, and the court moved to Blois. Charles VIII's widow Anne of Brittany now became Louis' wife. (Louis' previous incestuous marriage to Jeanne de France, daughter of his second cousin, was annulled by Pope Alexander VI's emissary Cesar Borgia.) To accommodate the family and retainers in their new eminence, the new king began the work of reconstructing his château.

Because of the frequent presence of the royal household at Blois, over the next two centuries the French royal family eventually created three châteaux in one here. Actually the people of Blois tend to insist on the formula 'three châteaux in one – plus one more'. They need the extra château, so as not to leave out the old feudal parts. These include the Tour des Oubliettes, which still boasts an old well; the thirteenth-century arcaded council chamber; and the Tour de Foix, rising 30 metres above the city, on top of which is a small seventeenth-century observatory.

To his medieval fortress-home King Louis XII added the graceful late gothic/early renaissance wing on the southwest side (which today overlooks gardens and the rue des Fossés du Château). Its facade is a most elegant blend of brick and stone. Here you spot the king's own curious porcupine device (the *porc-épic*) over the doors. The equestrian statue of Louis at the entrance is a nineteenth-century replica of an original destroyed at the Revolution.

Between 1515 and 1524 François I added a renaissance wing, a superb piece of Italian decor. In all probability the architect was an Italian named Domenico da Cortona. As well as bringing his own genius to the work, Domenico was ready to learn French ways, and his facade of Italianate loggias is topped by spirited, humorous gargoyles.

Finally Gaston d'Orléans, exiled to Blois by his brother Louis XIII, employed François Mansart to design the imposing, though unfinished classical southwest wing. It is sober, magnificent and (Flaubert added) chilly – though a kinder judgment might conclude that Mansart decided not to compete with the flamboyance of the rest but simply complement it in his own way. On the other hand, if Gaston d'Orléans had achieved his heart's desire he would have demolished everything and replaced it with a new building entirely by Mansart. Gaston's money ran out,

A renaissance monarch, King Louis XII; a detail of the château at Blois.

The startled porcupine, carved on the walls of the château at Blois, is in fact the emblem of King Louis XII.

but not before Mansart had been commissioned to redesign the chapel of Saint-Calais which dates from the time of Louis XII. (The panel behind the altar is by a pupil of Leonardo da Vinci, the less pleasing modern glass by Max Ingrand.)

The complexities of Blois château are to me most delightful seen all together, from the outside, and not on a guided tour from room to room. An excellent vantage point is place Victor-Hugo. From here you can best enjoy the perfect alliance between French gothic display and Italian renaissance grace revealed in the dormer windows of the wing built by François I. Walking along this side of the château you can see the varied delights of each contributing epoch gradually unfolding, and also how none of them really fit together.

No. 5 of this street (rue de la Voûte-du-Château) houses an unusual museum devoted to the celebrated magician of Blois, Robert Houdin, who died in 1871. Houdin created a 'theatre of fantastic evenings'. He went to Algeria, where his powers were considered greater than those of the local fakirs, thanks chiefly to his remarkably efficient pistols. The museum possesses these pistols, Houdin's magic wand, the incandescent lamp he invented in 1863, his revolutionary periscope, the transparent glass clock he made that seems to tell the time without works (the secret is electricity), his opthalmic instruments and much else.

Return to enjoy the garden of place Victor-Hugo, with its fountain, conifers and chestnuts, lilacs and rhododendrons, massive yew, willow and azaleas. The statue in this square happens to represent not Victor Hugo but Augustin Thierry, the historian of the Middle Ages, born at Blois in 1795. Its inscription reads, 'In the world there is something greater than material pleasures, than good fortune, even than good health, and that is devotion to knowledge.'

Hugo himself adored Blois. A few days after he arrived here as a young man he excitedly described it to Alfred de Vigny: a haphazard city displaying 'a thousand windows, all at once; a disorderly confused mass of houses, bell towers, a château, and a hill crowded with shadows.'

Across place Victor-Hugo the church of Saint-Vincent-de-Paul was built in the reign of Louis XIII. Inside are two monuments dedicated to Gaston d'Orléans in 1677 and paid for by his daughter Mlle de Montpensier. Saint-Vincent-de-Paul was once the church of the Jesuits of Blois, whose contemporary college next door is now the post office. At the other side of the church, across the road, is a charming

The abbey church of Saint-Lomer, Blois (which confuses the tourist by also calling itself the church of Saint-Nicolas).

building that now houses the city tourist office. It is known as the pavilion of Anne of Brittany. Surrounded today by nondescript modern buildings, this pavilion was once the orangery of the extensive gardens of the château.

From place Victor-Hugo rue Porte-Côte leads east. Just north, you find at No. 8 rue Saint-Honoré (at the junction with rue Porte-Chartraine) the Hôtel d'Alluye, built by a great survivor (or time-server), Florimond Robertet: known as 'the great minister' because he managed successfully to serve Charles VIII, Louis XII and François I one after the other as finance minister. The courtyard of his house has a double row of galleries, decorated with twelve terracotta medallions depicting the Caesars, and an extra one depicting Aristotle. The ill-fated Cardinal Guise of Lorraine lived here. Brother of the murdered duke, he had been made a cardinal in 1574 and Archbishop of Reims nine years later. A virulent persecutor of the protestants, he could hardly expect to escape the fate of his brother. On the day of the duke's murder the cardinal left this house for the last time, to be taken to prison and his death. His body and that of the duke were burned, and their ashes thrown into the River Loire.

No. 4 in the same street is another fine sixteenth-century hôtel with a splendid courtyard. Blois has much more of this kind to entrance the tourist who enjoys leisurely strolls. Return to rue Porte-Côte and turn right (southeast) along rue Denis-Papin, which soon turns south. Denis Papin was a Huguenot born in Blois in 1647 and exiled to Britain. Follow his street to rue des Trois-Clefs (where three gigantic keys indicate that this was once the street of medieval locksmiths), where you turn left to climb towards the cathedral of Saint-Louis. On the way to the cathedral do not miss on your left (at No. 3 place Saint-Louis) the merry

---

Blois seen across the Loire, its cathedral in the centre of the picture.

domestic building sculpted with fifteenth-century acrobats climbing up and tumbling down its timbers, the finest of those half-timbered houses in Blois that survived World War II.

Blois Cathedral was once dedicated to a Bishop of Chartres named Solenne, whose miracle-working relics attracted enough pilgrims and supplicants (and therefore money) to erect a fine romanesque church here. In 1677 the Sun King Louis XIV changed the dedication, not to himself but to his own patron saint, spurning the humble saint who had been venerated here for 600 years. The cathedral crypt, built to house Saint Solenne's bones in the 980s and extended a hundred years later, is still the most interesting part of the building. Its existence had been totally forgotten until it was rediscovered in 1928.

The rest of the cathedral of Blois was altered many times as the years passed. Today's west facade and impressive apse were created in the sixteenth century. The dome was added in 1609. Then a terrible storm of 1678 ruined much of the building, including its glass. The restoration was carried out in a deliberately archaic neo-gothic style, but the cathedral still looks odd, with no balance or form – an uneasy late seventeenth-century building on a medieval base – its strangeness emphasized, even symbolized, by the broken arch you meet on the left as you go in.

The bishop's palace, built behind the cathedral by Jacques Gabriel in the eighteenth century, is now the town hall. A statue of Joan of Arc commemorates her visit to Blois. From here you can look out over the old episcopal garden across the limes and chestnuts and beyond the River Loire, towards the cloister of Saint-Saturnin and for a panorama of the forests of Russy and Boulogne. The circular pavilion at the end of the terrace was built in the age of Louis XVI not long before the Revolution.

For a completely different aesthetic experience, walk east along rue du Haut-Bourg (north of the episcopal garden) across avénue Paul-Reneaulme and along rue Monin to find on the left at boulevard Carnot a monster church built out of reinforced concrete. Capuchin monks commissioned it in the 1930s from the architect Paul Rouvière, and his brief included two massive crypts and a nave capable of seating 1200 people. Notre-Dame-de-la-Trinité is dominated by a bell-tower with a carillon of forty-eight bells weighing in all seventeen tonnes. Its stained-glass windows are by such artists of the thirties and forties as Barillet, Hansen and Le Chevalier. The church houses sculptures by Lambert-Rucki. Those who do not warm to this epoch in religious architecture will ponder the significance of the relief on the facade by the brothers Martel, representing 'The Virgin Mary presenting the virtue of Humanity to the Trinity', and wonder when Our Lady intends to do so here.

Walk back to the cathedral square, where long, graceful curving steps ('*Les grands degrés de Saint Louis*') lead down to the old medieval and renaissance quarter of Blois. Much of this was grievously damaged in World War II. Much has been splendidly restored. I like to wander quietly through this sector of the city as far as the wide River Loire and its shapely bridge, pausing from time to time to sample the chocolates and candied fruits (*pistoles*) for which Blois is famed.

The eleven arches (some slightly pointed) of pont Jacques Gabriel were constructed between 1711 and 1724 by the architect whose name the bridge bears, and were partially rebuilt after World War II. From the northwest corner of the so-called rond-point de la Résistance, at the northern end of the bridge, rue Émile-Laurens takes you to a square with a magnificent, almost outrageous fountain, set here in the reign of Louis XII.

If you continue west along rue Anne-de-Bretagne and across rue Robert-Houdin you reach what is my favourite building in Blois: the abbey church of Saint-Lomer. (You can be misled if you lose your way by the fact that the church is also called Saint-Nicolas, for the abbey is no more, its buildings transformed into a hospital.) Its east end (including the transepts) dates from the early twelfth century, the rest of the stonework from the thirteenth (apart from one later chapel). In the nineteenth century two tall wooden spires were added to its massive square west towers.

Please do not be put off by the sadly ruined porch. Ignore the usual boring modernistic stained glass of the kind that can be seen in churches all over France. (This was created by Pierre Gaudin in 1959.) Inside, romanesque and early gothic architecture blend happily and harmoniously. The nave was inspired by Chartres Cathedral. At the east end four arches perilously support the dome. A stone altar-piece north of the choir is carved with scenes from the life of St Mary of Egypt. Of all the carved romanesque capitals, I like best the acrobats on the column to the south of the high altar (against the chapel dedicated to Joan of Arc), whose ever so slight vulgarity mocks the over-solemnity that too much piety can bring.

If the city of Blois itself is underestimated by tourists, the châteaux in its immediate vicinity are certainly not. You are spoiled for choice. No one visiting the Loire valley should avoid its greatest châteaux, but to avoid a surfeit I propose a tour of five: Chaumont, Beauregard, Chambord, Villesavin and Cheverny. All of them are within easy distance of Blois and each other. Over the years all have amassed historical anecdotes and personal stories of their owners and builders, sometimes happy, sometimes comical, sometimes tragic.

A twenty minute drive southwest from Blois, along the right bank of the river (by the N152 through Chouzy-sur-Cisse and then left across a bridge 425

The fifteenth-century château at Chaumont was made a little less formidable by the elegant alterations of the next century; but it still preserves its moat and drawbridge intact.

metres long called pont d'Escures) takes you as far as Chaumont-sur-Loire, on the borders of Touraine. Château Chaumont presents the two aspects we have come to expect in châteaux of this land: feudal and grim from one angle, elegant and welcoming from another. In the 1460s Charles d'Amboise inherited a feudal fortress here and set about its transformation into a renaissance château. I would not like to do without some aspects of the old fortress. Today a frisson of hostility is still suggested at Chaumont by the drawbridge and the cylindrical keep, as well as by the squat machicolated towers. The old fortress site has bequeathed to the château not only its defensive moat but also splendid panoramas over what is called hereabouts the garden of France.

In the 1550s Catherine de Medici bought the château for 120,000 pounds (in the currency of Tours). Here she brought an Italian necromancer named Cosimo Ruggieri, who claimed to be able to see into the future by looking into mirrors. Others said she hired him to cast spells that would throw her protestant enemy Henri de Navarre into a mortal illness. Catherine had hoped to obtain the château at Chenonceaux, but her husband preferred to see Chenonceaux in the hands of his mistress Diane de Poitiers. Diane had entranced Catherine's husband even before he became king. As a lady-in-waiting at the court of François I, she surpassed in wit and beauty even the king's official mistress, Anne de Pisseuleu, and utterly entranced François' son Henri.

Catherine waited till her husband's death and then, as regent, coldly forced Diane to give up Chenonceaux in exchange for Chaumont. In consequence the many initials flamboyantly carved on the walls and chimneys of Chaumont include not only the interlaced 'Cs' of Charles d'Amboise and his wife Catherine but also the 'D' of Diane de Poitiers.

Château Chaumont did not disappear from history after the death of these royal women. Napoleon exiled Mme de Staël here in 1810. This formidable protestant woman had inherited riches from her father, Jacques Neckar, finance minister to Louis XVI. At the age of twenty she was married to the Swedish ambassador in France. After Napoleon's seizure of power, she continually attacked his tendencies towards authoritarianism. When the two finally met, she insisted that men and women were equal in talent. 'Genius,' she declared, 'is sexless.' The emperor was appalled.

At Chaumont Mme de Staël completed her panegyric on the virtues of romantic Germany. And she immediately set up a salon, of literary geniuses of the calibre of Benjamin Constant, of German romantics such as Adelbert von Chamisso and August Wilhelm Schlegel, and of society women of the elegance of Mme Récamier. Constant managed to make love to both Mme de Staël and Mme Récamier, without apparently disturbing their close friendship. Sitting by his window in the château, von Chamisso wrote, 'In this old fortress have been housed the greatest spirits imaginable: the clever, dainty, cool, ponderous Schlegel; the fat, fiery Staël, with her light, happy, graceful movements; mild, pious Matthew Montmorency; beautiful, charming Récamier; sober, ugly, quiet, witty Sabran; the lovely, tender Bölk; a tubby, cold, harsh Englishwoman; a merry devil of a naïve, gay, tame, terrible, voluble Italian artist. . . .'

Later in the same century the Count of Aramon restored the whole château and refurnished it as it stands today. And in 1877 Prince Amédée de Broglie added some absolutely charming outhouses stabling no fewer than forty-two horses. His money and this château were the gift of Marie Say, heiress of the great sugar manufacturers (whose factory the British still come across as they are approaching Calais after their forays into France). She saw the château in 1875 and said, 'I want it.' Her elder sister replied, 'You are certainly rich enough to buy that.' So she did, for 1,706,000 francs. Two months later she and the prince were married. Here she entertained the amorous British monarch Edward VII, the Shah of Persia, the

Queen of Spain and the kings of Sweden, Portugal and Romania. She outlived her prince and in 1930 married for the second time. This time the groom was Louis-Ferdinand, heir to the Spanish throne. He was thirty-one years younger than his bride. Eight years later the château was sold to the French nation (for little more than Marie had paid), and a few years afterwards this splendid lady died, in a miserable lodging in Nazi-occupied Paris.

Six kilometres south of Blois, across pont Jacques Gabriel and along the D956, stands Château Beauregard. (A picturesque route from Chaumont-sur-Loire to Beauregard – provided you are a little bit careful over map-reading – is to follow the country roads that skirt the River Beuvron. Drive east along the D751 to Candé-sur-Beuvron, with its late eighteenth-century château. Continue east from here along the D7 to the charming fortified old village of Les Montils. From Les Montils the D77 meanders eastwards through the hamlet of Seur, until you reach Cellettes. Turn north here along the D956 and look for the signs to Beauregard.) A hunting lodge built for a friend of the poet Ronsard in the mid sixteenth century, Beauregard was transformed a hundred years later into a classical château. The architect, Jacques Androuet du Cerceau, created a graceful arcaded gallery, joining two similar but not identical wings. The gallery is topped by three classical windows, above which are three more dormer windows. The château interior was decorated by an Italian artist, Niccolò dell'Abbatte, then working at the French court. The courtier responsible for this transformation conceived the quaintly pleasing notion of commissioning Jean Mosnier to paint for this château 363 'portraits' of the great ones of French history, ranging from Philip of Valois to Louis XIV. Mosnier stunningly decorated the ceilings too. The château is also embellished with quite outstanding ceramics. Small wonder that Ronsard was inspired to write a poem in praise of 'sumptuous Beauregard'.

Then you drive east along the D33, to Chambord. If you have time, a more scenic route is to drive back to Blois and right along the south bank of the River Loire. On the opposite bank stand the château and ancient church of Saint-Denis-sur-Loire, followed by the château of Ménars, where Mme de Pompadour lived in the 1760s. Turn right down the D84 to Chambord, passing through the village of Montlivault – tiny, but boasting a splendid church, founded in the twelfth and finished in the sixteenth century.

The park of Chambord, $5\frac{1}{2}$ hectares of national game reserve, surrounded by 32 kilometres of walls pierced by six gateways, is roamed by deer, wild boar and humbler beasts. Straight ahead between the trees appear the turrets of the château. Chambord as you approach seems (in Châteaubriand's remarkable simile) 'like a woman whose hair streams in the wind, until closer you perceive that she is the fanciful network of her towers'. The white walls and slate turrets compose a château that at first seems surprisingly small, in view of its colossal reputation. Alfred de Vigny surmised that a genie of the lamp had transported an oriental château to this misty country out of the land of a thousand-and-one-nights; the château was, he wrote, 'royal, or rather quite magical'. The whole is entirely symmetrical, the interior decorations detailed and renaissance in contrast to the sterner, though still graceful exterior. Here Lully's music enchanted the court of the Sun King, and Molière produced his own *Monsieur de Pourceaugnac* and *Le Bourgeois gentilhomme* (*The Would-be Gentleman*).

The name of the architect of this masterpiece – with its 440 rooms – has been completely forgotten. The greatest wonder of Chambord is undoubtedly its monumental double staircase, so designed that one person can reach the top from the bottom while a second is descending, without either meeting the other, a piece of megalomaniac extravagance that, some say, needed the advice of Leonardo da Vinci in its construction.

From Chambord you take the D112 to Bracieux, a

Above **Beauregard: a hunting château turned princely residence.**

Right **The evening sunlight on Château Chambord.**

village blessed by two small rivers (the Beuvron and the Bonneure). The craftsmen of François I lived in and developed this village while building Château Chambord. Bracieux has preserved a lovely wooden market hall in its main square, with an outdoor staircase leading to the granary above. I very much like the nineteenth-century mosaic carpet of its church. The church itself was built in the late twelfth and early thirteenth centuries and boasts a stone altar-piece carved by G. Imbert in 1660 and a fine marble font of the same date.

Above **The superb renaissance basin in the courtyard of the château of Villesavin: note that the mermaid has two tails.**

Left **If, as Châteaubriand insisted, Château Chambord reminds one of a woman whose hair streams in the wind, here the hair is more than a little dishevelled.**

Below **King François I, magnificent prince of the renaissance, in a niche at Château Villesavin.**

Close by Bracieux is another celebrated château of the Loire valley, Villesavin. Villesavin, an exact contemporary of Chambord, is splendidly inspired by the Italian renaissance. This Italian influence is particularly visible in the lovely basin of carrara marble (carved with pretty cherubs and mermaids) in the courtyard, and in the medallions of the twelve Caesars which remind you of the Hôtel d'Alluye in Blois. Jean le Breton (François I's finance secretary) commissioned the château in 1537, as his own home when he was overseeing the building of Château Chambord. Its sixteenth-century pigeon-house is remarkable. Once the roof was covered in surplus lead from Chambord, but Napoleon requisitioned it and the present slate was substituted. Villesavin is a masterpiece, but such is the plethora of astonishingly fine châteaux in this part of the Loire valley that today Villesavin feels the need to attract visitors by housing a motor museum.

Even the magical Château Chenonceaux advertises its wax museum. And southwest of Villesavin, along the D102, Château Cheverny attracts custom by boasting a zoological park. Yet Cheverny certainly deserves a visit in its own right. A renaissance château about to turn classical, Cheverny was completed by Henri Hurault, Count of Cheverny, in 1634.

Its story began with a tragedy. In 1589 Hurault had married Françoise Chabot, the eleven-year-old daughter of an important French courtier. While Henri was serving in the king's army, Françoise dallied in the arms of a noble youth. Her husband caught them in flagrante delicto, killed the youth and offered his faithless wife the choice of death by sword or poison. She chose poison. After her death a surgeon took a five-and-a-half-month old son out of her corpse.

Hurault's crime was only lightly punished – by banishment to Cheverny. His second wife, Marguerite Gaillard, was a woman of great taste. Her own dislike of the old château of Cheverny and the unhappy memories it evoked in her husband led them both to create the present enchanting building. They engaged Jacques Bougier from Blois as the architect of their new home.

At Cheverny as Henri and Marguerite Hurault rebuilt it a majestic stone staircase (modelled on that of Chambord) leads to the so-called Chamber of the King, a room sumptuously decorated by the painter Jean Mosnier and hung with tapestries depicting the labours of Hercules. Mosnier also decorated the panelling of the dining room on the ground floor with scenes from the life of Don Quixote. The wealthy aristocrats of sixteenth-century France ranged afar for costly materials, and Château Cheverny proudly displays a state bed luxuriously covered in Persian embroidery. The smaller drawing room is hung with

Flemish tapestries, and boasts a Louis XV 'Chinese' lacquered commode. Its outbuildings include a trophy room containing over 2000 antlers from slaughtered stags, and its owners continue this sporting tradition by keeping a pack of English hunting hounds at the château.

As a curious parallel to the antlers in the trophy room, you can see the coats of arms of long dead members of the Hurault family in the twelfth-century church of Cheverny, which also boasts a twelfth-century porch, a sixteenth-century choir and a shady courtyard.

These five great châteaux by no means exhaust the seigneurial riches of the Loire valley. But from now on in this tour I find such great houses less overwhelming, not to say overweening. At the next two places along this route, Troussay and Fougères-sur-Bièvre, the great houses fit somehow more naturally into the environment, still fine but not totally dominating everything else.

Three kilometres southwest of Cheverny on the D52 you pass the renaissance manor house of Troussay, rendered more magniloquent in the seventeenth century by the addition of two wings (one tiled, the other slate-roofed). The right wing is especially imposing, the left-hand one more like a French farmhouse, with a couple of dormer windows. The ornamental doorway to the main house adds a little more class.

The countryside becomes nondescript and untidy as you follow the road on to Fougères-sur-Bièvre, to discover an extremely stern château, recalling a more ferocious age (Chambord without its renaissance trimmings), utterly dominating its village in a quite preposterous fashion. In the fourteenth century it was partly razed by the Black Prince. In 1427 Pierre de Refuge built the more habitable quarters around the old keep. After the Revolution the château served as a spinning mill. Today it belongs to the State, and you can walk into its courtyard to enjoy the contrast between its medieval towers, louring walls, and the finialled, renaissance dormer windows, decorated with coats of arms. The village itself is tumbledown, with a pretty church, housing stalls with sixteenth-century misericords.

Follow the winding forest road to Thenay and on to Pontlevoy. Here is another château with a chimney stuck oddly on the side of its pepperpot tower, as at Fougères-sur-Bièvre. The château gave the village its name, since Pontlevoy derives from *pont-levis*, i.e. drawbridge. As you walk past the château of Pontlevoy to the abbey church there appears over a doorway the inscription 'Religione et Patriae': the kind of ideology that has frequently buried our highest values under our basest, often subordinating the best impulses of religion to the needs of the powers-that-be.

This little spot has a rich past. Two monks of the monastery of Saint-Martin at Tours built themselves cells here in the ninth century. Guelduin, seigneur of Chaumont-sur-Loire in the early eleventh century, built a chapel in honour of the Virgin Mary at Pontlevoy after he had survived a terrifying shipwreck. The Benedictines founded an abbey on the spot in 1034, and set up a school here, which Louis XVI transformed into a military academy in 1776. Today it is an agricultural college. Benedictines also built the château. They needed it for their own defence, for brigands virtually demolished their abbey in 1422. (The monks successfully petitioned the Duke of Orléans to grant them a charter authorizing them to hire soldiers for their own protection!)

The present church and tower were built in the fifteenth century, for the old romanesque building was destroyed in a disastrous fire. Huguenots attacked the abbey in 1588 but spared the church. On either side of the altar are two reliquary busts of mitred bishops, each with a hole in his chest for the faithful to peer in and touch the bones inside, each neatly labelled with his name. One statue of the Virgin Mary dates from the foundation of the abbey: that in the fifteenth-century

chapel of Notre-Dame-des-Blanches. A fading wall-painting depicts St Martin cutting his cloak in two, the fortunate beggar dressed only in a flimsy diaper. The stalls date from the seventeenth century. Behind the church is the former abbot's residence, a beautifully proportioned eighteenth-century building with a terrace and formal garden.

The D764 leads from Pontlevoy to Montrichard, a thriving town, its square keep (built by one of Foulques Nerra's lieutenants in the early eleventh century) dominating the rest. (Climb to the top for some splendid views.) Just outside Montrichard, on 6 July 1016, the troops of Foulques and his ally Herbert Éveille-Chien ('Herbert the Watch-Dog') engaged the army of Count Eudes of Blois and his ally Gelduin of Saumur. Foulques was taken prisoner, and the soldiers of Blois and Saumur foolishly decided to rest. Suddenly the army of Herbert Éveille-Chien emerged from the forest and fell on their enemies, slaughtering or taking prisoner 6000 men.

Montrichard re-entered the history of the French nation in the fifteenth century. Here in 1427 Charles VII recognized as his natural sister Marguerite of Valois, the daughter of his father's mistress Odette de Champdivers. And on 8 September 1476 the future Louis XII (then aged twelve) and Louis XI's daughter, Jeanne de France (then aged nine), were married in the chapel of the château at Montrichard by the Bishop of Orléans. This chapel, now the church of Sainte-Croix, though much restored, still stands at the foot of the keep of Montrichard.

Just outside the town walls as you approach from Pontlevoy are fine renaissance houses. The fifteenth-century Hôtel d'Effiat takes its name from the Marquis d'Effiat who became seigneur of Montrichard in 1666. The extremely quaint (and very beautiful) eleventh-century church of Notre-Dame-de-Nanteuil stands not far from the railway station on faubourg de Nanteuil. In rue porte-aux-Rois is a hospice, one part fifteenth-century, the other sixteenth-century, with a pretty

renaissance chapel, and on the corner a leaning house made of wood, stone, brick and slate.

From here walk down rue du Poste and rue du Pont as far as the langorous River Cher, which is spanned by a bizarrely ancient bridge with eight arches all at different heights. On the far side of the river the arches are pointed. Did part of the bridge once fall down and have to be rebuilt? Where quai Jean-Bart meets quai de la République a plaque tells you that retreating German soldiers tried to mine the bridge on 2 September 1944. Men of the French Resistance saved it at a cost of six lives (five of them German lives).

The countryside around Montrichard produces succulent mushrooms, and the chalky cliffs house both troglodyte dwellings and welcoming wine caves, where visits are free, though few proprietors smile if you leave without buying a dozen bottles or so.

Cross the bridge of Montrichard that cost six lives and drive on to reach Faverolles-sur-Cher, whose extraordinarily pretty church is a fine example of Angevin gothic architecture. Inside is a multi-coloured renaissance altarpiece in which Jesus's parents sit in the most classy armchairs. As you leave you spot St Martin once again slicing his cloak in two.

From here travel south along the D764, watching out for the road that directs you left to the entrancing ruined abbey of Aigues-Vives. This is a ruin (to use the bench-marks of English romanticism) comparable to Bolton or Tintern Abbey in Britain. It stands amongst private houses and a mini-château. The tracery of the east end is bereft of glass. The romanesque doorway and painted romanesque columns hold up only the sky. A spire and a bell-tower are still intact. No longer do monks fish in the lake. No more do pilgrims come to beg St Giles to protect them from St Vitus's dance. Huguenots pillaged the abbey in 1562. The monks were driven out at the Revolution. Today it is dangerous to penetrate the ruin, but the last time I picnicked there a black goat was tethered to a column, nonchalantly keeping down the grass.

From Aigues-Vives I would make my way eastwards to Saint-Aignan-sur-Cher, not so much for its château or its church as for its remarkable bird sanctuary. All three are in fact a delight. A hundred and forty-four steps lead up to the renaissance château, which François I rebuilt on the foundations of an earlier one erected by Count Eudes I of Blois (some of which – including the round tower to the northwest and the

Château Gué-Péan, a few kilometres east of Montrichard, has remained virtually unchanged and certainly unspoiled since it was inspired by the Italian renaissance.

Left **The 'Maison du Passeur', built in the sixteenth century on the old bridge at Montrichard to control the traffic across the River Cher.**

square tower to the south – still survives). The church is romanesque and early gothic, tall and extremely slender, with a fine square bell-tower and wall-paintings in the crypt (including a roundel of a very spirited Lamb of God, trotting like a pony). It also boasts a fifteenth-century chapel dedicated to Our Lady of Miracles, its vault decorated with powerful sixteenth-century paintings of St Michael fighting the dragon and weighing souls.

The bird sanctuary in the park du Beauval here is filled with feathery creatures of virtually every colour and kind. You find the park by taking the D675 from the village of Saint-Aignan-sur-Cher signposted towards Limoges/Le Blanc. Five hectares of wood-lands, meadows and gentle running waters nurture a collection of over 1000 birds that is unique in France, allowing them to breed naturally and to live safely. Living together are parakeets and parrots, cranes, pheasants, ducks and flamingoes, toucans and birds of prey, all cared for, and open to view every day of the year from 10 am until sunset.

Saint-Aignan-sur-Cher has a goodly number of medieval and renaissance timbered houses. Cross the River Cher here and continue driving east to the picturesque fortified town of Selles-sur-Cher. Its name hints at the cell by the river that St Eusice, a hermit from the Dordogne, built for himself in the sixth century. Eusice was a counsellor of kings, and when Childebert consulted him before doing battle against the Visigoths in 542, the monarch built the saint a church, in which Eusice's bones were kept after the saint's death. An abbey founded on this venerable spot was pillaged by the Huguenots in 1562 and restored in the nineteenth century. On the facade is a fascinating double frieze, the lower part depicting scenes from the

Inside the eleventh-century church of Saint-Aignan, even St Joan of Arc seems overawed and temporarily subdued.

Old Testament, the upper scenes from the lives of Christ and of St Eusice.

Selles-sur-Cher is defended by a jolly château built of brick and stone, the château itself protected by a circle of water. The countryside of Selles-sur-Cher is irrigated not only by the River Cher but also by the Fouzon and Sauldre, and the Berry canal passes through the town. A tour of the château unfolds magnificent sculpted chimneys, fine furniture and a lovely polychrome decor.

Renaissance steps lead to the shady square and ancient church at Saint-Aignan-sur-Cher.

Drive northeast to Romorantin-Lanthenay. From the name of this town legends have arisen about its Roman origins, even that it was founded by Julius Caesar. The truth is that the town first appears in history in the twelfth century as a fief of the Counts of Blois. The Black Prince took Romorantin-Lanthenay in 1356, but the French soon took it back. Thirty years later Froissart reported the marriage celebrations here of the daughter of the Duke of Berry.

The château at Romorantin-Lanthenay was rebuilt by Jean of Angoulême between 1448 and 1467. Here in 1499 was born Claude de France, who married the future king François I only fifteen years later. And when the town survived the worst horrors of a plague in the years 1584–5, the thankful citizens attributed this to St Roch, who became their patron saint. In 1626 they built a chapel in his honour where you can still see the ex voto thanksgiving for their deliverance. St Roch also, they say, greatly encourages the grapes grown around this town.

Romorantin today welcomes tourists, with fine campsites, a skating rink, and a museum devoted to the history of sports-car racing. If you stay here any length of time, do not forget to visit the entrancing Château du Moulin, built amidst blue waters in two quite separate parts.

Drive directly back to Blois from Romorantin-Lanthenay to explore the territory to the northwest of the *département* of Loir-et-Cher. From Blois the D766 runs due west to Molineuf, traversing lovely forests. At Molineuf in 1511 Florimond Robertet built a château that was a pioneer of renaissance architecture in the Loire valley, but today it is in ruins. The road

now runs northwest to Herbault, a village with a pretty tree-lined square and a pink château that has been totally restored in our own century.

From here take the D108 through Saint-Amand-Longpré – where the church of Saint-Amand is nineteenth-century gothic and the church of Saint-Pierre is eleventh-century romanesque. Further on lies Lavardin. Lavardin is a charming little village, curiously shaped because of the river and the lie of the land. The old priory of Saint-Genest, built in the twelfth and thirteenth centuries, is now the town hall. In 1188 the château of Lavardin defeated the combined attack of Henry II and Richard the Lionheart. At the end of the sixteenth century Henri IV decided that so impregnable a château were better demolished, and so all that remains are some ramparts and part of a keep, from which there are splendid panoramic views.

At Lavardin try to get into the church. When it is unlocked, the entrance to Saint-Genest-de-Lavardin is by the rickety side door, not from the west end. The roof is barrel-vaulted. The fascinating wall-paintings are in a perilous condition. On the pillar just as you go in you can make out St John, with his poisoned chalice. St Antony appears with a poor cripple, on the south side, just before the chancel. On a pillar opposite, a slender Jesus is baptized. Over the apse is Christ in Majesty with the symbols of the four Evangelists, or rather three of them, for one has totally deteriorated. The chancel carvings include romanesque figures and curly patterns. The crude carving of the Madonna and Child on a capital on the north side of the choir is reputed to be one of the earliest romanesque representations of this theme.

Ruined châteaux now flank this whole stretch of the Loir. Cross the ancient narrow bridge spanning the river by Lavardin and drive $2\frac{1}{2}$ kilometres to Montoire-sur-le-Loir. In the surprisingly wide and empty place Clemenceau stands the flamboyant church of Saint-Quentin-lès-Trôo, drastically restored in the last century and looking today as good as new. The

A fortified church in the picturesque village of Lavardin that saw great battles in the Hundred Years War. Today the church is more at risk from neglect than from pillaging soldiers.

Above **The square and church of Saint-Quentin at Montoire-sur-le-Loir, both quiet save on Sundays when people go to church and on Wednesday afternoons and Saturday mornings when they go to market.**

Right **The beautifully restored twelfth-century church in the troglodyte town of Trôo. Note the massive buttresses against the apse.**

interior is simple and beautiful. Ronsard was prior of the abbey of Saint-Gilles (to the west of the town, by the river). To see his abbey church today, with its fearsome wall-paintings of scenes from the Apocalypse, ask for the key at the hardware store opposite. On 24 October 1940 Adolf Hitler met Marshal Pétain on the railway station at Montoire-sur-le-Loir, a rendez-vous chosen because a long tunnel nearby would have provided cover in case of an attack from the air.

Six kilometres west from Montoire-sur-le-Loir along the D917 lies the remarkable troglodyte town of Trôo. The road to the old part of the town is well signposted,

---

Vendôme was a major staging post on the pilgrimage route to Compostela, and the figure carved on the left of this fifteenth-century house is the patron saint of pilgrims, St James the Great. Note his pilgrim's staff, bag and hat. His hat sports a cockleshell – the symbol of Compostela itself.

meandering in and out of the place, through fields and occasional vineyards until it suddenly narrows at the ruined ramparts. Trôo in fact seems at first a charming but nondescript place until you come to the fortified mound, on top of which is the twelfth-century collegiate church of Saint-Martin with a central tower athwart the rest of the building. Here is a beautifully restored and superb romanesque doorway, with carved birds hungrily pecking carved grapes. The carved capitals inside are equally delightful: Daniel in the lions' den being licked by the friendly beasts; two stonemasons and a peasant with an axe; centaurs with crossbows; all in bizarre twelfth-century poses. On the north side of the apse the beggar once again confronts St Martin.

Behind the church is a deep well, whose echo is renowned. Here are seats, shady beeches and a chestnut tree, as well as an orientation table and a telescope. You can see as far as 40 kilometres beyond the château and winding river.

To see the troglodyte dwellings at Trôo you must go on foot down the steep path that leads from the mound. These fascinating underground houses are all privately owned and inhabited, often faced by very pretty front walls and gardens. The hillside here is tunnelled like Gruyère cheese, part naturally, part the creation of men and women over centuries, providing places of refuge in times of war and civilized homes in times of peace.

From Trôo drive back to Montoire-sur-le-Loir and then northeast for a climax to this tour at Vendôme. The road runs parallel to the river, overhung with cliffs. Suddenly at Les Roches-l'Évêque, not quite 4 kilometres out of Montoire-sur-le-Loir where the D917 turns right towards Vendôme, the cliff rises absolutely sheer over the river and you can see more troglodyte homes in the very rocks themselves, beautifully fashioned houses with windows and patios of stone.

Vendôme holds back its treasures. From whichever end you approach it, you drive through desultory

The statue of Marshal Rochambeau, the romantic hero of Vendôme.

tabacs and bars, modern flats and camera shops. The magical part is the pedestrianized city of Pierre de Ronsard, who was born here in 1524. Ronsard's earliest verse celebrates the beauty of his city and its region:

'O happy land,
Haunt of the muses
With your gentle, calm light
Whatever the season, whatever the sky,
So long as heaven blesses me
This little nook of countryside
Shall entrance me above all others.'

A hint of glories to come at Vendôme might be gleaned from the former church of Saint-Jacques, now a state-owned gallery displaying the work of local artists and craftsmen. The barrel-vaulted roof is held together by great tie beams, monsters' hands clutching each side of the beams. The pulpit is still there and usually music is playing. Not far away is another lovely church, La Madeleine, again barrel-vaulted, angels as well as beasts holding up the painted roof, with renaissance stained glass, and a gothic organ on the balcony.

The town hall and public library of Vendôme, with its magnificent courtyard, was once a college run by priests of an order founded by St Philip Neri. (The college was established in 1623 by the son of Henri IV and Gabrielle d'Estrées.) Balzac was educated here and in his day it was named the Lycée Ronsard. Over its archway is a bust of Ronsard (set there in 1934) and inside the archway on the right is a bust of Balzac. An entry displayed in the old school register records: 'Balzac (Honoré) . . . Boarder. Conduct: good. Character: slow. Promises well.'

The novelist later recalled his days here in his novel *Louis Lambert*. As he remembered, the stench of the cooped-up pupils almost made him ill. Each morning everyone washed in the same two pails of water. 'The place, being cleaned but once a day before we were up, was always more or less dirty. In spite of numerous windows and lofty doors, the air was constantly fouled by the smells from the washing-place, the hairdressing, the lockers, and the thousand messes made by the boys, to say nothing of their eighty close-packed bodies. And this sort of *humus*, mingling with the mud we brought in from the playground, produced a sufficiently pestilential muck-heap.' Punishments were horrific. What Balzac remembered with great pleasure was eating. The Oratorians were enlightened enough to allow the boys to talk at table, and a complicated system evolved for exchanging a piece of food one boy disliked for another he liked. A boy wanting more lentils instead of dessert would call out 'Dessert for lentils!', and soon someone down the table would accept this gastronomic barter. The boys kept pigeons, played cards and bought sweetmeats by

stealth. In the end, Balzac concluded, he remembered with delight, 'the eccentric pleasures of that cloistered life'.

Walk from here to the tourist office in the Hôtel du Bellay – it belonged to the poet's cousin – across a fine park (where a notice on a plane tree tells you it was planted in 1759). Then stroll to the main square of Vendôme, the place Saint-Martin. In this square is the tower of St Martin's church, all that remained when the rest fell down in 1856. Here too is a statue of Rochambeau, Marshal of France, looking for all the world like a romantic hero. Rochambeau was born at Vendôme in 1725 and fought for the Americans in their War of Independence. He formulated new military tactics which were enthusiastically developed by Napoleon. He died in 1807, having narrowly escaped execution in the Revolution. Not everyone else was so fortunate. In 1796 the ultra-revolutionary Gracchus Babeuf was executed here in the place d'Armes for conspiring against the more cautious leaders of the French Revolution.

All of which is merely a prelude to the astonishing revelation, first left beyond the statue of Rochambeau, of the flamboyant facade – a series of white, stone flames – of the abbey church of the Holy Trinity, Vendôme. This facade is the greatest achievement of a brilliant early seventeenth-century architect, Jean de Beauce.

Holy Trinity Church was founded by Geoffroy Martel (who rebuilt the now ruined château at Vendôme) in 1035 on the site of an older one. (A separate twelfth-century bell-tower stands 79 metres high beside the present building.) The church tower is 40 metres high, the spire another 35 metres. Successive generations of builders kept to the original plan of a Latin cross but added their own particular genius to the whole. Double flying buttresses support the building, complex and rational all at once. The interior is narrow, elegant and simple. The choir stalls were carved in the fifteenth century. Walk round the high altar to examine the seventeenth-century woodwork and, set in the modern glass of the apse, a Madonna and the Infant Jesus, surrounded by angels, in glass dating from 1440 – the oldest stained-glass image of the Virgin Mary in Christendom.

The D957 takes you speedily southeast back to Blois, through Villeromain (whose name indicates the old Gallo-Roman town from which it grew), where the church was first built in the eleventh century and boasts three sixteenth-century windows on the south side. Lots of neolithic tools have been discovered around here, and if you stop a little further towards Blois at La Chapelle-Vendômoise, make sure you see the fine prehistoric dolmen de la Pierre Levée, which dates from the same era.

It is scarcely believable that the stone flames on the flamboyant church of the Holy Trinity, Vendôme, are not flickering.

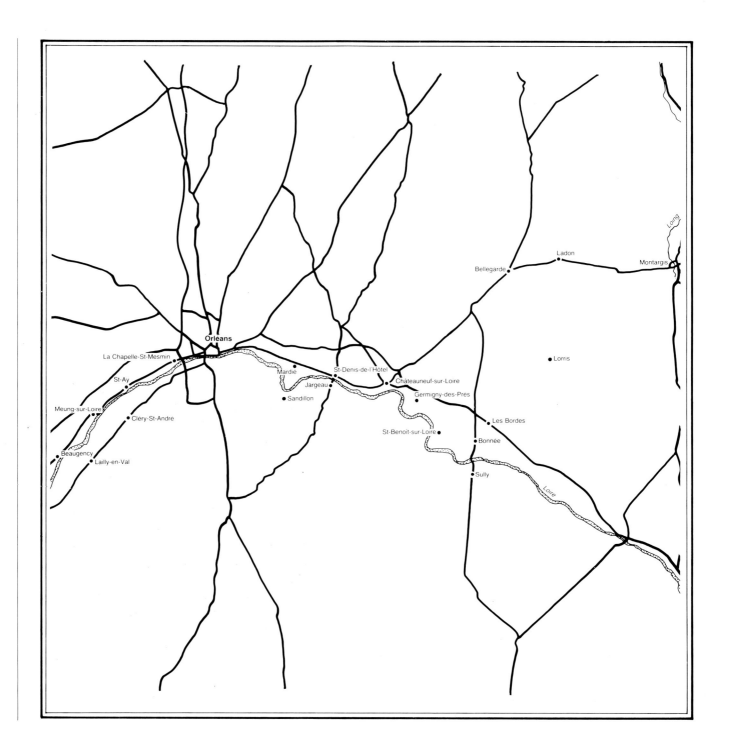

5
Savagery and Tranquillity

Orléans – La Chapelle-Saint-Mesmin – Beaugency
– Cléry-Saint-André – Montargis – Saint-Benoît-
sur-Loire – Jargeau

It should be clear that I am assuming that my readers will tour the valley of the Loire by car. Many great nineteenth-century travel-writers relied on the railway. Most of them hated it. The Reverend Augustus J. C. Hare shall speak for them all:

'Many English tourists in France, especially English ladies, find much to complain of in their railway journeys; indeed, it would often seem as if the railway companies did everything in their power to prevent people from using their lines. Smoking is now allowed in *all* the carriages. It is true that, nominally, passengers can prevent anyone from smoking by an appeal to the guard, but he shrinks from interfering if possible: or, if he takes any notice, the complaining passenger's position in the carriage is thenceforward almost untenable.'

Augustus Hare continued:

'Worse even than the smoking, and the spitting, which is its constant concomitant, are the hot water tins, which may be welcome, especially in the north, during the cold days of December and January, but which are equally forced upon the miserable traveller in the most broiling days of April, or under the hottest Provençal sunshine.'

Today French inter-city trains are among the best in the world, almost always on time, air-conditioned, comfortable, well-serviced. A very reasonable alternative to motoring all the way to the Loire valley is to travel there by rail and hire a car when you arrive. This is especially convenient if you wish to explore the *département* of Le Loiret and its regional centre, Orléans, for around Orléans is an extraordinary richness of buildings, gardens and history – and yet the area involved is also compact, demanding very little in the way of driving.

Orléans is a much underestimated city, with fine buildings, parks and music. Some 'minor' buildings offer a rare treat. Opposite the station, for example, on the right-hand side of the rue de la République, stands the Hôtel Moderne, a marvellous art nouveau building dated (on its facade) 1902. To my knowledge no guidebook has ever deigned it a mention. Another unsung building close by is the massive (though still unfinished) late nineteenth-century church of Saint-Paterne, just to the right of the station (facing rue de la République) along boulevard de Verdun. One Saturday evening I arrived by train and was walking to my hotel when I heard music from the organ of this church. Excitedly I rushed inside – or nearly so, for the great old doors of Saint-Paterne have been replaced with virtually invisible plate-glass, and I smashed

151

blindly into it. For some moments after staggering into the church I sat oblivious even to the notes of its superb organ, or the eighteenth-century paintings Saint-Paterne inherited from a defunct convent.

The city achieved its greatest historical fame through Joan of Arc. In 1429 she inspired an army that miraculously delivered Orléans from the English. When at first Joan asked King Charles VII for men whom she might lead to relieve the city, her request was opposed by a large group at court, led by the king's favourite La Trémouille. He put forward the view that the maid was either crazed or an imposter. She was accordingly sent to Poitiers, to be examined by theologians. After three weeks of gruelling interrogation, they reported that they could find nothing against her and that Charles ought to take the maid into his service. So a special standard was made for her, emblazoned with a representation of God the Father to whom two kneeling angels present the fleur-de-lys, and with the words 'Jesus: Maria'. In white armour Joan led the army against the English. Though herself wounded in the breast by an arrow, she and her men successfully captured the English forts around Orléans and raised the siege.

This was Joan's finest hour. She herself would have pressed on to rout the English entirely, but La Trémouille and others wanted to negotiate. The king was wise enough to allow Joan and her ally the Duc d'Alençon one short, entirely successful campaign in the Loire valley, which ended when they crushingly defeated the English general Sir John Fastolf at Patay. Charles VII was crowned at Reims on 17 July with the maid, holding her standard, at his side.

But still he vacillated. His failure to support an attack on Paris brought about the maid's first repulse by the English. At this battle an arrow entered her thigh and d'Alençon had to drag her to safety. On 14 May 1430 she was attempting to relieve Compiègne and had actually entered the city when the drawbridge was idiotically raised after she had led her men out on a sortie. Joan was dragged from her horse by the enemy and became the captive of the Duke of Burgundy.

From him she was bought by the English. Chained to a cell in Rouen she was forbidden to wear men's clothing. Cross-examined publicly and privately about her visions, she refused to retract. Only once, before a huge crowd in the cemetery of Saint-Ouen, did her nerve momentarily fail, and she made a faltering retraction. Her captors led her back to her cell. There she once again defied them by donning men's clothing and once again declaring that the voices she had heard truly came from God. She was condemned as a relapsed heretic. At eight o'clock on the morning of 30 May 1431 Joan of Arc, not yet twenty, was burned at the stake and her ashes thrown into the River Seine. Twenty-five years later the Pope overthrew the verdict of her judges and rehabilitated the maid. On 16 May 1920 she was declared a saint.

Virtually every year since the day she first entered Orléans the citizens have celebrated the feats and memory of St Joan on the 7th and 8th of May – the 8th being the day she rid the city of the English and became the illustrious 'maid of Orléans'. At noon on the 7th the maid's standard is presented to a vast crowd assembled outside the town hall. The following day the bells of the churches ring out. The cathedral and its square are illuminated. Solemn services of thanksgiving take place. In the afternoon a jubilant procession crosses the whole city. And in the evening a military celebration of the saint's exploits takes place, in the place du Martroi.

Walk south from the station along rue de la République and you reach this square. Here is a splendid equestrian statue of the maid of Orléans, created by Denis Foyatier in 1855. The helmeted saint, sword in her right hand, sits crosswise on her steed

---

Domestic tranquillity near Orléans: a house with shutters and roses.

Statue of Joan of Arc, giving thanks to God for her victory, place du Martroi, Orléans.

like a man, not side-saddle like a woman. Foyatier has depicted her giving thanks to God for her victory – hence her downcast sword – yet ready if necessary for further battle. Two panels on the sides of this monument bear reliefs by Vital-Dubray depicting scenes from the saint's life. (Foyatier had produced a couple of panels of his own, but the city fathers decided they were too expensive.)

One April Fool's Day here I spotted that the French do not, after all, take their national saint with undue solemnity. 1 April in France is known as the day of April fish, when people surreptitiously stick cut-out paper fishes on each other's backs, crying merrily '*Poisson d'Avril*' when the victim spots the sticker on his or her coat. On this particular April Fool's Day, hanging under the belly of Joan's steed in the place du

Martroi was a huge cardboard *poisson d'Avril*.

The square is a noble piece of town planning, slightly diminished by some unworthy modern buildings. Happily, Hitler's bombs in 1940, the attacks of the US airforce in 1943 and the allied bombardment of 1944, which destroyed much else in Orléans, mostly missed the old chancellery that stands on the west side of the square, though fire bombs did cause some damage to this lovely building – a gift to the city from the Duke of Orléans in 1759. It has been scrupulously restored. Flanking the opposite side of the square is the chamber of commerce, intelligently built in 1865 in the same style as the chancellery.

Walk to the right of the chancellery past the post office into place Charles de Gaulle. Here is the timbered house where Joan of Arc lived for ten days in 1429 (or rather, a meticulous reconstruction of the fifteenth-century building that Hitler's bombs did manage to destroy). The house today shelters souvenirs, sketches and documents of the maid. Place Charles de Gaulle is the centre of a number of charming fifteenth- and sixteenth-century houses. One of the earlier date (situated a little way to the left down rue Tabour), with a lovely interior courtyard, is now dedicated to the memory and relics of Charles Péguy.

Péguy was born at Orléans in 1873 in the utmost poverty. His mother supported her son by mending broken chairs. Charles was brilliant, and won a scholarship to the Lycée in Orléans and then to the École Normale Supérieure at Paris. No doubt as a result of his childhood experiences, he became a passionate socialist. His writings dream of a city where there shall be no private wealth and no injustice. He was an equally passionate Christian, and poured out his ideas in philosophy and in poetry, as well as in a glittering fortnightly journal which he founded and edited. As a true son of Orléans he revered the memory of St Joan of Arc and wrote a socialistic play about her in 1897, followed by one of his masterpieces: a philosophical poem called *Mystère de la charité de Jeanne d'Arc* (*The mystery of the charity of Joan of Arc*).

Charles Péguy was forty-one years old when World War I broke out. He believed (in his own words) that 'those who die in a just war are blessed'. On the first day of the Battle of the Marne he was standing looking through field-glasses when an enemy bullet pierced his brain and killed him.

The Péguy museum in rue Tabour possesses the manuscripts of nearly all his poems and writings. A bust of Péguy can be seen at Orléans in place de Bourgogne (rue de Bourgogne leads off rue Tabour). By a grisly coincidence, a piece of shrapnel from World War II has damaged it precisely where the bullet of 1914 killed him.

From place Charles de Gaulle follow rue Notre-Dame-de-Recouvrance south towards the River Loire. Along a little street to the left you see a late gothic tower and a chapel known as Notre-Dame-des-Miracles, virtually all that remains of a church where the maid of Orléans gave thanks before a statue of the Virgin Mary for her success in 1429. This particular statue had been in Orléans since the fifth century, attracting countless pilgrims because of its alleged miraculous powers. In 1562 the Huguenots threw it on a fire. World War II destroyed almost all the rest of the church.

On the left as you continue down rue Notre-Dame-de-Recouvrance you pass Hôtel Toutin, built with a fine colonnaded courtyard in 1540. This elegant building is often wrongly called the house of François I. Toutin was in fact the dauphin's valet de chambre.

A few paces further on is the church that gives this street its name, a fine early sixteenth-century building with contemporary stained glass in the apse depicting scenes from the life of Christ. It has often been pointed out that, although the church commemorates the time when Jesus's anxious mother found her lost twelve-year-old son sitting talking with the elders in the Jerusalem Temple, these stained-glass scenes un-accountably omit this episode in his life.

In a few metres you reach the riverside, at quai Cypierre where the bourgeoisie of seventeenth- and eighteenth-century Orléans became rich by trading in sugar and by manufacturing candles. To the left is a superb arched bridge spanning the Loire, flatteringly dedicated to the British King George V, though it was built by an architect and engineer named Robert Soyer in the mid eighteenth century (after the collapse of the old medieval bridge). Its present name symbolizes the British-French collaboration during World War I.

The lovely arcaded rue Royale, which runs north from here to place du Martroi, was begun in the same century as the bridge, but never finished until after World War II – another example of the enterprise of present-day Orléans. In 1791, in rue Royale, Orléans, William Wordsworth fell in love with Annette Vallon, who bore his child. To my mind its shop windows are quite as elegant as the most glamorous of Paris.

Elegant rue Royale reminds me that you can not only shop but also eat and drink well in Orléans. The gastronomic specialities of the whole region include fine pâtés and *rillettes*. As elsewhere in the Loire valley, the chefs here mix meat and game with fruit. Tender sheep are bred in this part of the Loire valley and appear on menus as *gigots de mouton*. During the season for game you can be offered haunch of venison (*gigue de chevreuil*) or of stag (*cerf*), rich slices of wild boar (*cuissots de sanglier*), or a fricassée of rabbit or hare in wine. As a dessert, try *pithiviers aux amandes*, a delicious, flaky-pastry almond cake.

As for cheese, the variety is extremely enticing. In summer and autumn try the varieties of cows' milk cheese called *pannes cendré*, *bondaroy au foin* and *olivet bleu*. You can find early *olivet bleu* in the first weeks of spring. Over centuries the local farmers have developed skills for guaranteeing that the supply of cheese does not run out in winter, so that in the Orléans region even at Christmas you can confidently ask for *olivet cendré* or *patay*.

In 1644 John Evelyn warned Englishmen to remain

The Maid of Orléans recognizes the dauphin: one of Vital-Dubray's panels on the plinth of Joan of Arc's equestrian statue in the place du Martroi, Orléans.

sober in Orléans. 'The Wine of this place is so grosse & so strong,' he noted, 'that the Kings Cupbearers are (as I was assured) sworne never to give the King any of it: But it is else a very noble liquor, & much of it transported into other Countrys.' The only Englishmen willing to stay here for long were, in his view 'such as can drink & debauch'. Alas, the phylloxera blight of the late nineteenth century destroyed most of the Orléans wine industry. Today the city is more renowned for its excellent wine vinegars. But you can still feast here on wines from elsewhere in the Loire.

Continue along the river bank past rue Royale and along quai du Châtelet to view what I consider an extremely creditable new market hall with a fine wooden roof. At the corner of quai du Châtelet a mark incised high on the wall indicates the astonishing height reached by the waters when the Loire flooded on 2 June 1856. The detail appears yet more remarkable on those August afternoons when the river seems almost dried up, with vast expanses of shoals and cars parked on islets in the middle. Yet, as Mme de Sévigné once wryly observed, 'the River Loire does tend to flood'. The autumn waters of the Massif Central suddenly swell the stream and the Loire is transformed, if not quite into a wild beast, into a torrent that even two powerful dams have found hard to tame.

Take now rue Sainte-Catherine leading north from the market hall. This street joins rue Ducerceau, where you find yourself walking between the Hôtel Cabu on your left and the old town hall on your right. Hôtel Cabu was built by the lawyer Philippe Cabu in the mid sixteenth century, and this lovely renaissance building now houses the historical and archaeological museum of Orléans. It is perhaps only here, among its Celtic and Gallo-Roman treasures, that you realize how truly ancient this city is.

Hôtel Crénaux across the road is an altogether more complex building, an amalgam of parts built in the fifteenth and the sixteenth centuries, dominated by its bell-tower and by the lovely facade dating from the very early 1500s. When I first started visiting Orléans the Hôtel Crénaux housed the museum of fine arts. This has been transferred to a building north of the cathedral, which I find a pity, for fine works of art are better housed in fine works of architecture. Still, connoisseurs will find much to delight them in this rich collection, which includes Tintorettos and paintings by Vélazquez as well as nineteenth-century

The unique, wedding-cake towers of Orléans Cathedral, designed by Louis François Trouard, rise above the city.

French masterpieces. Those particularly interested in local connections will make directly for the room devoted to Max Jacob who spent the last years of his life near Orléans at Saint-Benoît-sur-Loire.

As you walk up rue Sainte-Catherine turn right at rue Jeanne-d'Arc. This street, passing the Joan of Arc centre on the left, leads directly to the much maligned cathedral of Orléans. Proust described it (wrongly) as the ugliest in France. I think many find it hard to appreciate this cathedral simply because a lack of historical perspective means that they are looking for the wrong thing. Though clearly a gothic building, the present cathedral of Sainte-Croix at Orléans was begun only in 1601, when Henri IV inaugurated the replacement of an old cathedral almost entirely destroyed by the Huguenots. (The Pope had made this a condition of receiving Henri as a catholic.) Even then building proceeded slowly until King Louis XIV lent his authority to the project, and later the genius of the architect Jacques-Ange Gabriel was brought into play.

The cathedral of Orléans was finally completed only in 1829. I find it interesting to try to spot the variations in styles in what remains a complex, yet harmonious and delicate gothic building. If you need convincing, walk outside round the east end, and let its buttresses and proportions make their effect. From here it is hard to imagine the disaster of 1904, when the sanctuary collapsed, hurtling twenty tonnes of stone down onto the high altar.

Inside, the chapels of the apse remain from the old cathedral and date from the late thirteenth century. Two other bays in the nave – built in the mid sixteenth century – were retained from the older, venerable building. The transepts clearly date from the epoch of Louis XIV (from 1679, to be precise), since their rose windows incorporate the device and quaint motto ('*Nec pluribus impar*', 'Not unequal among many') of the Sun King. The west front was not begun till 1767, inspired by the designs, subsequently often modified, of Gabriel.

I find the two wedding-cake towers quite magical – who cares if nothing like them has been seen before or since on a gothic cathedral? Much of the credit for them goes to an architect named Louis François Trouard. The device of building the bottom tier slightly curved and the upper one round seems to me entirely successful. Trouard also decided that the west front needed a more gothic aspect, and redesigned the portals. Then, twenty-nine years after the cathedral was supposedly complete, Émile Boeswillwald added his *morceau* of nineteenth-century gothic in the form of the central spire, 104 metres high.

Inside Sainte-Croix the organ was similarly built over three centuries. Jules Hardouin-Mansart and Jacques-Ange Gabriel designed the stalls. Finally, in 1893, stained-glass windows were made for the aisles, illustrating the life of the maid of Orléans. Altogether the soaring interior of the cathedral of Sainte-Croix, Orléans, measures 41 metres across, 136 metres in length and 32 metres from ground level to the topmost arches.

Northwest of Orléans Cathedral stands Hôtel Groslot, the town hall of the city. It dates from the mid sixteenth century. Here, when the Estates General were meeting in December 1569, King François II died. Until the Revolution this was the home of the governor of Orléans. The wings of the building were added in 1790 when the hôtel became the town hall. In front of the hôtel a statue of Joan of Arc by Marie d'Orléans stands bareheaded, without her gauntlets, meditating or praying. Behind her is a lovely, slightly crumbling stone balustrade below the brick-faced hôtel (with four caryatids holding up pediments on either side, the two monumental women doing the work effortlessly, the men finding the task slightly more of a strain).

Inside the cathedral is a fairly cloying tomb of Monsignor Dupanloup, Bishop of Orléans from 1849 to 1878. Félix-Antoine-Philibert Dupanloup was certainly a remarkable man, who rose from an illegitimate birth to become a great prince of the Church. He is said to have converted Talleyrand in 1838. A pioneer in the education of women, Dupanloup was elected a member of the French Academy in 1854. A tireless and emotional preacher, he once raised 30,000 francs for the relief of Irish poverty by means of a single charity sermon. Then he took up ecclesiastical politics. A passionate defender of the temporal power of the Pope, he nonetheless vainly opposed the declaration of papal infallibility at the Vatican Council of 1870. Dupanloup was more successful in his equally passionate opposition to Rationalism, and one of his last public acts was to stop the French government officially recognizing the centenary of the cynic Voltaire in 1878.

He also loved Orléans. Many higher positions in the Church were offered him, yet he preferred to remain here as bishop for twenty-eight years. And he it was

A caryatid from the renaissance Hôtel Groslot, now the town hall of Orléans.

who introduced at Rome the cause for the beatification of the maid of Orléans, Joan of Arc.

Rue Dupanloup, named in the bishop's honour, takes you past the eighteenth-century episcopal palace behind the cathedral (now the municipal library, including a fine collection of manuscripts and *incunabula*) to rue Saint-Euverte, which in turn leads to the church of Saint-Euverte. This imposing building retains its twelfth-century pattern, but subsequent depredations (including damage at the siege of 1429 and attacks by Huguenots) have necessitated many restorations and rebuildings, so that the church today even boasts an unexpected seventeenth-century dome.

What these often fragmentary church buildings achieve is to rescue for us the ancient history of Orléans, often seemingly lost after the battering of World War II, when virtually the entire centre of the city and more than 3000 buildings were destroyed. Euverte was Bishop of Orléans in the sixth century. A previous bishop, even more celebrated, was St Aignan, who led the citizens of Orléans to partial victory against the troops of Attila in 451. If you walk from the church of Saint-Euverte south along boulevard Saint-Euverte, right along rue de Bourgogne and left again along rue de l'Oriflamme, you reach what remains of the church of Saint-Aignan, after the siege of Orléans by Joan of Arc and the Wars of Religion.

You are again close to the river. Gardeners, amateur or professional, can find themselves close to paradise simply by driving across the River Loire at Orléans. A drive right, along quai du Châtelet and then south across Pont George V leads you to the first of two horticulturalist's delights: the botanical gardens that the Orléans society of apothecaries founded in 1640. The gardens are open throughout the summer, and you reach them after you have crossed the bridge by turning immediately right along quai de Prague.

If instead of turning right at the southern end of the bridge you drive 8 kilometres south, you reach another

superb (and this time recent) creation: the floral park of La Source. In 1964 it was decided to make a flower garden out of 30 hectares of woodlands around the source of the Loiret – that curious basin out of which a miniature whirlpool rises. These mild waters today nourish exquisite pink flamingoes. Other unexpected animals in the floral park at Orléans include emus, wild sheep and deer, as well as a fine collection of exotic birds. The park has been designed to flourish almost all the year round: tulips, azaleas, hyacinths, rhododendrons and 600 varieties of iris in spring; petunias, geraniums, salvias, begonias and over 100,000 roses in summer; dahlias and chrysanthemums in autumn; rock plants all the year round. Here – presided over by a seventeenth-century château – are lakes and pergolas, artificial mounds and brick paths imaginatively filled with shrubs and flowers. These gardens nurture medicinal and herbal plants, and succour experimental species. A gardeners' advice centre is on hand, and, for those who like to ride precariously around the park, a miniature railway. This utterly entrancing garden is open to the public from 1 April until mid November.

A good time to leave the city in order to explore the riches around Orléans is just before lunch, for within 5 kilometres, at La Chapelle-Saint-Mesmin, is a lovely spot for a picnic. To reach it, start on the north side of the River Loire and drive west along the quayside, bearing left towards Blois and taking the N152. You pass old tumbledown barns and new functional buildings. At the village of La Chapelle-Saint-Mesmin itself, turn left towards the signposted old people's home (*Maison de Retraite*) and then along rue Saint-Honoré until you reach the place du Bourg. The square, sheltered by plane trees, is in my experience usually quite deserted. It boasts one shop, selling cakes

---

Poppies in the lush meadows of the Loire valley around Orléans.

and bread. This is the France of yesteryear, a few metres off the awful, dusty beaten track. Down rue de l'Église is the eleventh-century church, and as you walk towards it, there is the river, with an esplanade, seats for your picnic, and a view in the distance of the cathedral of Orléans.

This entrancing spot has attracted men and women since prehistoric times. One kilometre upstream at Monteloup is a prehistoric site where, as we know from excavated piles of bones and antlers, reindeer hunters lived 17,000 years ago. Polished stone axes discovered at La Chapelle-Saint-Mesmin itself are witness to the activity of the neolithic tribes who once lived here.

The locals still assert that when the Celts lived at La Chapelle-Saint-Mesmin the natural cave in the hillside here was a sacred spot for Druidic rites. Then the Romans came and built their rural villas in the neighbourhood and little forts to keep the natives in order and to control the traffic along the river. In the fourth century St Mesmin converted them to Christianity. When his uncle St Eusice looked for a solitary spot where he could end his days away from the corruptions of the world, he and his nephew set up a hermitage here. In spite of the extreme austerity of their lives, they did not remain alone for long. Other hermits soon joined them, forming a flourishing monastic community along the banks of the Loire, even though each monk for the most part still lived a life of seclusion in his own cell.

Their lives, it appears, were threatened at this time by a fearful dragon, who had taken up his abode in the former Druids' cave. The seventeenth-century Orléans historian Symphorien Guyon takes up the tale:

'In those days on the bank of the River Loire was a huge and horrible cavern, the haunt of owls and suchlike creatures. In this pestilential place was born a terrible dragon, which lived off stinking, corrupt flesh. Eventually the beast grew so huge that the cavern was too small for its bulk. It emerged, and by its venomous, stinking breath and its unbearable stench tainted all the neighbouring land and so infected the air that the little birds that flew around it fell dead to the ground. In short, the desolation was so great that the place would have become a desert had not divine providence sent a speedy remedy.'

Divine providence acted through St Mesmin. He crossed the river with a blazing firebrand in his hand, and flung it at the monster, which burned to death.

Mesmin died in 520, insisting that his fellow monks bury him in the dragon's cave. This unusual tomb soon attracted countless pilgrims. Criminals and escaped slaves found sanctuary here, and this right ultimately created the charming village that exists today. It happened thus. A nobleman of Orléans named Agylus (or Ay) had a slave who committed some grave fault and fled in terror to Mesmin's cave in order to escape his master's rage. Not one of Agylus' servants dared enter the cave in pursuit of the miscreant. The inflamed nobleman decided to risk violating the sanctuary himself. As he rode up, his very horse baulked at the task. Agylus dismounted, and as he approached the cave, sword in hand, was struck with a terrifying paralysis. He begged the dead saint's forgiveness, vowing that if he were healed he would build a church by the river. Mesmin cured Agylus, and the nobleman built here La Chapelle-Saint-Mesmin, around which grew up the little village of the same name.

In the peace of today it is hard to envisage the often violent subsequent history of La Chapelle-Saint-Mesmin. The present church is not the one built by Agylus, for the Normans many times pillaged the monastery and devastated the church. Whenever the monks rebuilt it, they took care not to scrap the old materials, including stones and bricks once used by the Romans.

For centuries, this small hamlet could not be left in peace. The Huguenots went so far as to burn the venerable bones of Mesmin himself, scattering his ashes to the winds. The Loire often flooded the foundations of the church, and in the seventeenth century Henri IV's councillor Sully decided to safeguard it by building a powerful wall to hold back the waters. In so doing, his engineers unwittingly walled up Mesmin's cave, which by this time had been enlarged and held up by two massive ancient romanesque pillars. (The cave was rediscovered only in the nineteenth century.) At the Revolution the church was used first by that curious and short-lived sect known as 'Theophilanthropists', before being deconsecrated and used as a warehouse for saltpetre.

Finally the villagers got their church back and slowly began its restoration – very slowly, in fact, for the church at La Chapelle-Saint-Mesmin was not fully restored until Monsignor Dupanloup came to bless the completed work in 1864. The bell-tower was added four years later. A pneumatic organ was installed in 1897, and deemed sufficiently valuable to be meticulously restored eighty years later.

Somehow none of this repeated restoration seems to have spoiled the church. Even the modern glass is (unusually) good, depicting Mesmin healing the sick, building monasteries and so on. Miraculously, the eleventh-century west facade of the church survived every calamity. And this facade boasts a remarkable pre-romanesque porch, with club- and lozenge-shaped stones still perfectly, magically interlocking.

Leave La Chapelle-Saint-Mesmin by driving left beyond the church along rue du Four and then right back to the N152, which takes you along the right bank of the river through Saint-Ay (where the choleric Agylus built a hermitage and where Rabelais lived in the mid sixteenth century) to Meung-sur-Loire. At the right season the route here is lined with sunflowers.

A home in the timber and brick style typical of this region, in contrast to the stone houses elsewhere in the Loire valley.

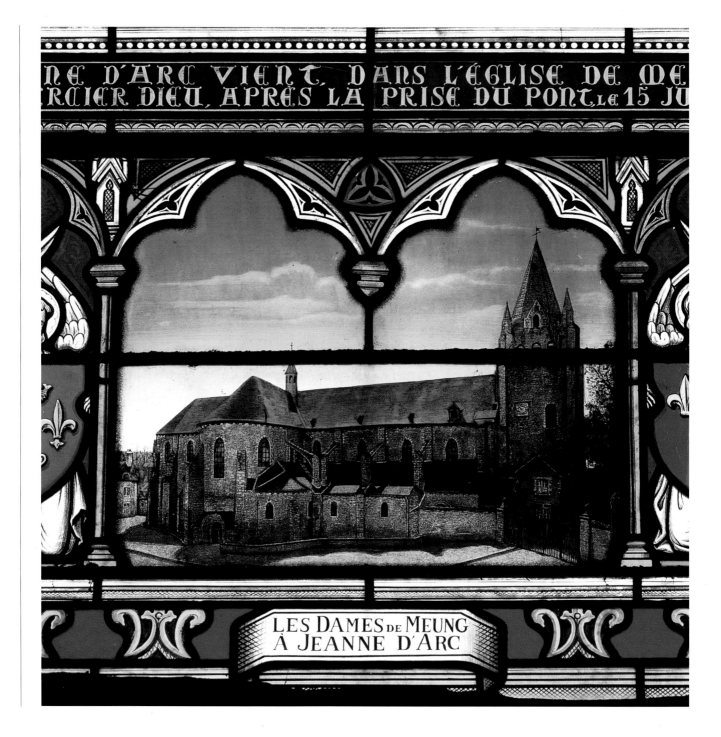

At Meung-sur-Loire, rivulets (known locally as 'Mauves') used to drive water-mills as they tumbled into the Loire. Along rue du Docteur Henri-Michel you reach the old covered market. The village *boulangerie* and *pâtisserie* is timber-framed, and on the corner of rue des Remparts is another timbered house with strange fish-monsters carved on its frame.

The painter Ingres lived in the 'Maison du Change' at Meung-sur-Loire between 1843 and 1866. Till the eighteenth century its château served as the palace of the bishops of Orléans. The poet Jehan de Meung was born here in 1240. (His statue in the place du Maupas was erected in 1949.) Jehan added some 18,000 verses to the *Roman de la Rose*, which Guillaume de Lorris had left unfinished. He ended the poem with a lament over his own lameness.

But the most important poet to spend time here was Villon. In 1461 the Bishop of Orléans imprisoned him in the dungeon of the château, pending the poet's execution. Villon escaped death only because Louis XI stayed at Meung-sur-Loire and in an act of general clemency pardoned the poet-criminal. Follow the signs for the château along the medieval layout of the streets of Meung-sur-Loire. Basically the château dates from the thirteenth century, though it has been many times restored and its present chapel was built in the eighteenth century. Entrance is by way of a double archway that seems almost flat (with an empty niche above it). One arch lets in carriages and horses; a separate arch is wide enough for pedestrians.

A wall connects the château with the church of Saint-Liphard (another sixth-century hermit), whose tower is as squat as the streets of Meung-sur-Loire are narrow. The thirteenth-century nave is supported by

The squat-towered church at Meung-sur-Loire, depicted in a stained-glass window dedicated by the women of the town to Joan of Arc.

impressive flying buttresses, two of them splendidly joined at right-angles to each other.

Though its three-leafed choir is unique in the region, Saint-Liphard at Meung-sur-Loire is to my mind curiously barren inside, with a tiny organ, a little font set in the wall, Liphard's late seventeenth-century reliquary (depicting him as bald and bearded), and a frightful fresco painted in 1943 and depicting the saint standing on the river bank next to his monastery. Two capitals add some merriment: one carved with a juggler, the other showing a couple fighting. Outside, the architecture is filled with delights, from the dog-toothed romanesque doorway on the north side to the many grimacing faces peering down at you from the medallions carved high on the walls.

Another 7 kilometres along the N152 and you reach Beaugency. As you approach you can see on the left the squat old keep next to the church spire – again the might of the State and the grace of the Church hand-in-hand. Turn left, running along the ancient walls of Beaugency into which people have built houses and workshops, to reach a charming old stone bridge, dating from the eleventh century, which ambles for twenty-one irregular arches across the river. Such a long bridge, men reasoned, could scarcely have been built by human hands, and the legend arose that the devil gave it to the town in exchange for the soul of the first person to cross it. The wily mayor of Beaugency sent across a cat, which sent the devil into such a rage that he kicked one of the arches slightly out of line.

The ancient town wrinkles on your right, with an iron portcullis defending Château de Dunois. You enter the town through a round arch with an ancient clock-tower. In 1152 the now half-ruined keep of the château at Beaugency housed a melancholy ecclesiastical council which annulled the marriage of the cousins Louis VII and Eleanor of Aquitaine on account of their consanguinity. The real reason was that he was a saint and she a hot-blooded heiress. Even on a crusade together they had quarrelled. The king lost not only a

Below The ancient, irregular bridge crossing the River Loire at Beaugency.

Right The beautiful renaissance town hall of Beaugency, built in 1526.

wife but also half his realm, for Eleanor made over her vast inheritance to her next husband, Henry Plantaganet, future king of England, and thus involuntarily started the Hundred Years War.

Ironically enough, an earlier ecclesiastical council held at Beaugency had excommunicated King Philippe I for repudiating his queen in order to marry Bertrade de Montfort, Countess of Anjou.

The ancient and superb rectangular tower of the château – all that remains of the first to be built here – is a perfect example of an eleventh-century military keep, 36 metres high and flanked with buttresses. The rest of the château, with its polygonal staircase-tower, belonged in the fifteenth century to Joan of Arc's ally Jean de Dunois. It boasts an extremely pretty oratory, with representations of the coat of arms of the Dunois family and their motto '*Cor mundum crea in me Deus*' ('God create in me a pure heart'). Today it is the home of the regional museum of folk art. Beaugency is not content with this one museum, and its ornate renaissance town hall houses Gobelin tapestries and local embroidery.

The scars of war can be seen not only in the ruined keep at Beaugency but also in the abbey church of Notre-Dame close by. Huguenots set fire to its twelfth-century roof in 1567, and the present wooden vaults (built in the 1660s after the building had lain open to the elements for ninety-five years) do not quite fit. The medieval stained-glass windows were sadly destroyed by the bombs of 1944, making way for the present anodyne glass of 1952.

If you did not picnic at La Chapelle-Saint-Mesmin, lots of picnic places reveal themselves after you have crossed the bridge at Beaugency and are driving along the D19 towards Lailly-en-Val (where in 1920 a seventeenth-century château was beautifully restored and is now an old folks' home). This is great hunting and fishing country. Turn left at Lailly-en-Val and drive 7 kilometres along a road lined with poplars (the D951) to Cléry-Saint-André. I find it extraordinary

that King Louis XI and his second wife Charlotte of Savoy lie buried in this tiny, typical Loire valley village, even though it was his own wish that his last resting-place should be here (for he believed that Our Lady of Cléry-Saint-André had granted him the victory over the English in 1443 at the siege of Dieppe); but then, I find it amazing that little Cléry-Saint-André possesses such an enormous flamboyant basilica of a church.

A previous church (of which the massive square tower remains) was destroyed by the English during the Hundred Years War. Three impressive elaborate doorways decorate the west facade of the rebuilt church. The interior is tall, bare and spacious. The only stained glass is that enhancing the windows of the apse. This was a pilgrims' church, part of the route to Santiago de Compostela, and a late gothic chapel on the south side of the basilica contains a spectacularly animated wooden statue of St James, patron saint of pilgrims, carved and painted in the sixteenth century, a cockleshell on his hat, his beard curly, his moustache flowing, his hair long and beautifully brushed. The brother-architects Gilles and François de Pontbriand came from Brittany in the second decade of the fifteenth century to build this superbly vaulted chapel. Here also are two other remarkable statues, both sculpted in the sixteenth century: a beautiful, smiling Virgin, and a langorous, almost completely naked St Sebastian.

Quite different and very beguiling is the triangular vaulting which the architect Simon de Val built over another chapel here in the late 1460s. This Dunois chapel (alas locked) contains the family tombs of Jean de Dunois, Joan of Arc's faithful ally.

Pilgrims en route for Compostela came to Cléry-Saint-André to pray before a mystical statue of the Virgin Mary, said to have been discovered in a thicket in 1280 by a peasant (and the original reason for building this vast church). Alas the Huguenots burned it, and the present oak statue on the high altar is a sixteenth-century reproduction. The canons' stalls in the basilica of Cléry-Saint-André display comically wild faces carved under renaissance misericords.

But this is not why we are here. The verger takes you to the north aisle. To the right of the seventh arch a rusty door is let into the floor. It opens to reveal below, in a recess of their coffin, the trepanned skull of Louis XI and the slightly rosier skull of Charlotte of Savoy. After this, to learn that this basilica of Notre-Dame at Cléry-Saint-André also possesses the heart of Charles VIII is decidedly an anticlimax.

Walk out of the church, relishing as you go the flamboyant tracery of the west window, and then slowly walk round the building to admire the lovely south portal, the sturdy, powerful buttresses of the south and north sides, and the marvellously delicate buttresses of the apse.

The D951 leads you back to Orléans, in order to explore the rich treasures to the east of the city. Châteauneuf-sur-Loire, on a great bend in the river, is the first, a gem of a town, spacious and irregular. The charming seventeenth-century château (or what was left of it after the depredations of 1803) has become a maritime museum – a memorial to a centuries-old way of life on the River Loire that the railways killed. Mansart built its lovely stables and orangery. Le Nôtre set out its park, which boasts an alleyway 900 metres long planted with giant rhododendrons, all of them flowering in May and June. Much of the park you see today must be attributed to the work in 1821 of the celebrated botanist Huilard d'Hérou, who was inspired by what he had seen in English gardens to plant over thirty different species of trees here.

Châteauneuf-sur-Loire, with its swimming pool and camping sites, has set itself to attract tourists without destroying its own integrity. It has, I think, succeeded. Its market hall – upheld by three rows of eight wooden pillars – retains a rustic charm. The town also boasts a second, cast-iron, open market hall. Why does it need two?

Close by, the bell-tower of the church is joined to the fifteenth-century house of God by two arches. The church itself was badly damaged during World War II and has (among some regrettable concrete restorations) a new, fine, arched wooden roof and modern stained-glass windows (by Archepal). Inside is a thought-provoking tomb: that of Louis Phélypeaux, Lord of Vrillière and secretary of state to Louis XIV, who died aged eighty-two in 1681, having loyally served the King of France for forty-two years. Two grisly skeletal

The statue of Neptune fittingly graces Châteauneuf-sur-Loire, with its museum of long-gone days when sailing boats tacked up and down the river.

Tomb of Louis Phélypeaux (1598–1681) in the church of Saint-Martial, Châteauneuf-sur-Loire. While the grisly skeletons gnash their teeth, an angel gently raises Louis from the grave and points the way to heaven.

green, white and gold. One is inscribed 'Ave Maria' and as you walk out you see another inscription 'IHS'. An excellent incised tomb to François de l'Hôpital, seigneur of Soisy-aux-Loges and chamberlain of the Duke of Orléans till his death on 24 November 1427, is a reminder of the days of St Joan of Arc. (The slab has been taken up from the floor and placed against the south wall of the south chapel.) Look out for the painting of St John, attributed to the artist Mignard. It is said to be a portrait of Mme de Montespan as a child.

The entertainingly complex château of Bellegarde stands off the main square (place Charles Desvergnes), approached through monumental wrought-iron gates. Surrounded on three sides by a moat, its red-brick and white-stone front, its turrets and its solid keep look slightly bad-tempered in the peaceful Bellegarde of today. Walk round the back to look at the monumental staircase and square Doric columns holding up a balcony, as if this side of the château had vainly tried to appear a little gentler. Every August the grounds of this château are the setting for a festival of art organized by the town. The pretty town hall (Hôtel de Ville) on your left as you leave the grounds was built in 1727. Its three exposed bells surmounted by a weather vane still chime the hours and quarters.

To reach Montargis drive east through Ladon, with its double-roofed market hall (a legacy of the seventeenth century) and through Saint-Maurice-sur-Fessard, which boasts a charming mill and an old dovecote. Montargis is a little Venice. Its walls are bathed by the waters of the River Loing and the Briare Canal (constructed in 1604). Inside the walls, houses

caryatids (one half-rotted) flank his memorial. His son Balthasar erected the tomb in 1686 as (in the words of the inscription) an eternal thanksgiving to his father's love.

Bellegarde, a sleepy town with old houses and second-hand shops, lies directly northeast from Châteauneuf-sur-Loire, along the N60. The nursery gardens of Bellegarde are famous throughout France for their roses. Do not forget to walk into the church. Its romanesque west facade is particularly rich. Inside is a fine, barrel-vaulted wooden roof (dating from the twelfth century) tied with cross-beams painted in red,

The château at Bellegarde, which Nicolas Braque built in the fourteenth century, has not lost its defensive aspect, even though later owners (especially the Duke of Antin, Mme de Montespan's son) added gentler touches – such as the dormer windows and graceful pavilions.

The romanesque doorway (with dog-toothed patterns) of the church of Our Lady, Bellegarde.

overhang rivulets crossed by 126 bridges. Montargis is a town of medieval streets – rue Gudin, rue du Loing, rue du Four-Dieu – flanked by lovely old houses, some still with their medieval courtyards. Two early seventeenth-century convents, their nuns long departed, now serve as the hospital and the law courts.

And here was invented that scrumptious delicacy made of grilled almonds coated with sugar-water and vanilla which we call 'praline'. Praline was created in the reign of Louis XIII by the inspired chef of the Duke de Plessis-Praslin. The historic site of this invention stands in the central square of Montargis (place Mirabeau), to the right of the church of St Mary Magdalen and the risen Christ. The house, known as 'Praslines Mazet', was in fact restored in 1920, and is inscribed 'AV MARECHAL DVC DE PRASLIN'.

The exterior of the church of the Magdalen is fairly boring, apart from the apse, with an impressive seventeenth-century porch, and the bell-tower and spire which Viollet-le-Duc added when he restored the building in 1860. Inside is a superb renaissance choir built by Androuet du Cerceau.

Apart from its praline, Montargis is celebrated most of all for a remarkable dog. The story runs that during the reign of Charles V the dog's master, the chevalier Abri, was murdered by a certain Macaire. The sole witness was the animal, which watched over its master's corpse for three days before making its way to the château. There the terrified Macaire attempted to kill the beast, which leapt at him and felled him. The murderer and the witness confronted each other at a public trial. Macaire was found guilty and executed. Walk from the church of the Magdalen about 200 metres down rue du Loing (across the Briare Canal, with picturesque locks) until you reach the town hall (Hôtel de Ville) on the right-hand side. Its gardens contain a dramatic bronze sculpted by Gustave Debrie in 1874, depicting the dog savagely leaping at Macaire, whose face is contorted with agony, his hand futilely clawing the air.

A more peaceful memorial in this garden is the delicate pointed arcade which dates from the twelfth century and was brought here from the Château des Salles at Lorris to the south.

Montargis is a very busy spot. Its position, dominating great thoroughfares from Paris to Lyons and from Nantes to Nancy and situated where the Orléans and Briare canals meet the River Loing, has created an expanding economy. Amidst all the bustle it is odd to think that Montargis was the birthplace of the great mystical quietist Mme Guyon. Yet each day at lunchtime everything is suddenly quiet again. And just outside the town there are still 4000 hectares of forest, threaded by countless paths and alleyways.

The road to Lorris (back towards Orléans on the N60 and then left along the D961) traverses part of these forests. Lorris was the birthplace of the Guillaume who wrote the first 4000 verses of the *Roman de la Rose*. No more than a shadow of its former self, this town was once a favourite hunting post of the kings of France, who built a château and surrounded it with ramparts, all of which have almost completely disappeared. Yet the place remains charming, with its twelfth-century church (boasting a splendid organ-case, built in 1500), surrounding lakes, a sixteenth-century renaissance town hall, and a market hall ancient enough to have been destroyed by marauding English and rebuilt in the mid sixteenth century. Among the lakes, well worth seeking out is the sandy-shored Étang des Bois to southwest, where tourists swim and sail when the weather is warm.

The road southwest from Lorris crosses the D952 at Les Bordes and joins the D948 at Bonnée (where an ancient fountain, dedicated to St Antony, is reputed to cure any sickness for those who have enough faith). This road leads due south to the splendid château of Sully, impeccably washed by a tributary of the River Loire. The fourteenth-century martial aspects of this château were softened 200 years later by the additions of Maximilien de Béthune, better known as Sully (the title he took when made a duke in 1606), who became Henri IV's financial secretary and wrote here a famous treatise on the proper economic regulation of the state. In the eighteenth century Voltaire was banished to Sully in 1716 for publishing a satire on the regent, Philippe of Orléans. He was, he wrote, a thousand times happier here than before his exile.

We are however making for one of the most celebrated churches in the whole of the Loire valley: Saint-Benoît-sur-Loire, northwest of Château Sully on the way to Châteauneuf-sur-Loire. The great church is unmissable as you approach its tiny village. How could such an apparently insignificant spot possess such a huge basilica – long, high and beautiful, the apse (as so often in this region) slightly off-centre, so that the modern east window seems to be peering round a corner at you? The answer lies in the power exercised by the relics of a saint in the Middle Ages.

Around the year 650 Benedictine monks founded a monastery here, south of the village of Fleury (now called Saint-Benoît-sur-Loire) and on the banks of the River Loire. Over a hundred years previously, the founder of their order, St Benedict, had died and been interred in his own monastery of Monte Cassino north of Naples. When Monte Cassino was devastated by the Lombards, the monks fled, leaving the saintly relics behind. In 672 the monks of Fleury conceived and carried out a daring plan to steal these neglected bones and bring them over 1000 kilometres from Italy to their new monastery in France. Naturally enough the Italian Benedictines denied that their founder's relics had been neglected, yet (in spite of legal proceedings and episcopal threats), the bones remained in their new home.

The illustrious relics attracted visitors and lavish gifts. Saint-Benoît-sur-Loire became famous and rich. Whenever the Normans raided the territory, the monks fled with the saint's corpse to the safety of Orléans. When the Normans left, the monks returned and rebuilt. The abbey became one of the most famous in western Christendom, establishing countless dependent houses (including Pershore Abbey in Worcestershire in England) and bequeathing bishops and archbishops to the Church. The monks saw themselves as leaders of contemporary monasticism. In 1020 Abbot Gauzlin built a monumental tower with no fewer than fifty columns (now known as the Porch-Tower), 'an example,' as he put it, 'to the whole of Gaul'. Gauzlin also brought here from Italy flagstones of polychrome marble, Byzantine work of the fourth or fifth century AD. And when in 1026 a fire burned down much of their abbey church, the monks of Saint-Benoît-sur-Loire took the opportunity of building a yet more splendid house for Benedict's bones. The new

Left The medieval château which Henri IV's financial secretary Sully transformed in the early seventeenth century into one of the most entrancing of the Loire valley.

Above The winding river as it approaches the ancient abbey of Saint-Benoît-sur-Loire.

175

crypt to house them was completed by 1067, the romanesque double choir and sanctuary by 1108, the nave and lower aisles by 1150.

Gauzlin's tower was designed to represent the heavenly city, New Jerusalem. In the form of a square with twelve doors – three facing west, three facing east, three facing north, three facing south – it is sculpted with scenes from the biblical vision of St John the Divine: the four horsemen of the Apocalypse; the damned emerging from a pool of fire; the great candlesticks that represent the seven churches; war in heaven. Other sculptures represent St Martin and the beggar, the flight into Egypt and so on. One capital (on the northwest side) bears the inscription 'VNBERTVS ME FECIT' – a reference perhaps to the master-mason who oversaw the building of the tower.

Some of the carved capitals inside the abbey church are equally brilliant in conception and in execution. Satan and a six-winged seraph dispute over a human soul, represented by a sexless little body. An angel, just in time, stops Abraham's sword slaying his blindfold son, who sits innocently cross-legged on an altar. Lions menace a horned man whose arm is linked with a fearful woman.

Joan of Arc and Charles VII made a pilgrimage here at the end of June 1429, probably to venerate the fourteenth-century alabaster statue of the Virgin Mary (now in the north transept) as much as St Benedict. The monks survived the Wars of Religion, though protestant soldiers pillaged the abbey. (You can still see the damage they did to the wonderful sculptures of the north doorway.) At the Revolution the Benedictines were finally driven out. Their successors returned in 1944. The modern monastic cells are on the south side of the church, and at times of service you can today join the monks in the crypt as they chant the daily office.

From 1924 Saint-Benoît-sur-Loire was the home of the Jewish poet and painter Max Jacob, friend of Picasso and Modigliani, Cocteau, Braque and Apollinaire. His house is in the main square to the right of the café. In this village he wrote that 'colour and light are not what create the beauty of the countryside, but the Spirit.' Although he had been converted to Christianity in 1915, he was arrested by the Nazis in 1944 and died in a prison camp at Drancy. His body was brought back and lies interred at Saint-Benoît-sur-Loire.

The road now delightfully runs alongside the River Loire all the way to Germigny-des-Prés. Here the Carolingian church is infinitely less elaborate and imposing than the abbey church of Saint-Benoît-sur-Loire, but it is nonetheless a jewel. Built in 803, it seems deceptively simple until you note the complexities of its interior arches. The windows are made of alabaster, exactly like those of the Byzantine churches of Ravenna in Italy. And this connection with the churches of the Adriatic is not fortuitous, for Charlemagne brought here what is certainly unique in France: a ninth-century mosaic from the Emperor Theoderic's palace at Ravenna, which depicts gleaming golden angels swooping in awe over Moses' ark of the covenant.

The church at Germigny-des-Prés houses some beautiful medieval gothic statues. Two, both from the sixteenth century, are to my mind by themselves beautiful enough to persuade anyone to visit this spot. One shows the Virgin Mary teaching Scripture to her aged mother. The other is an intensely moving Pietà, sculpted in Burgundy. When I first visited Germigny-des-Prés I knew the church also possessed an exquisite tiny reliquary, made in the twelfth century out of *champlevé* Limoges enamel. I asked the lady verger if she would show it to me (it is locked away in the

---

South of Sully and Saint-Benoît-sur-Loire the countryside grows yet richer, as this lush scene near Saint-Florent reveals.

vestry), and as an extra treat she also got out a magnificent eighteenth-century antiphony book.

Germigny-des-Prés is no more than 4 kilometres from Châteauneuf-sur-Loire. On the way back to Orléans it is worth veering left at Saint-Denis-de-l'Hôtel (where both château and church date from the sixteenth century, though the church is much restored) and following the signs that take you across the suspension bridge to Jargeau. Here on 12 June 1429 Joan of Arc won a bloody victory over the English. When a huge stone thrown by the enemy crashed down on her helmet, many thought her lost, but the maid sprang valiantly to her feet again – an incident commemorated by a bronze statue (by Lanson), erected in 1895 in the place du Martroi.

The church has a square tower with arches that have been filled in over the centuries. The outside is stern, the interior very beautiful, with a romanesque nave, and an Angevin gothic choir with nineteenth-century woodwork incorporating stations of the cross. Connoisseurs of sickly piety will respond not only to these stations but also to two stained-glass windows (of particularly fine colour), one dated 1888 and depicting St Bernardette perceiving the Virgin Mary outside her grotto, the other dated 1893 and showing Christ revealing his sacred heart.

A market is still held every Wednesday outside the church, spilling out into the open air of the square, where the chestnut trees offer their shade. The market hall of Jargeau is a splendid iron building of 1884. As you walk down the main street (rue Porte-Berry – twisting, picturesque and unsuited to modern traffic), notice the old houses transformed into shops; a restored arcade; a fish-shop and a shoe shop opening directly onto the street in medieval fashion. Over the

Medieval imagination peopled the banks of the River Loire with all manner of dragons and evil beasts.

centuries some of the corner-stones, shaped long before machine tools, have begun to lean slightly (as, for example, those supporting the shop on the corner of rue Saint-Michel).

The citizens of Jargeau enjoy life. Their Shrove Tuesday carnival is a celebrated jollity. The town is the seat of the quaint 'confraternity of the knights of the pork sausage' – 'Confrérie des Chevaliers du Goûte-Andouille' – and a pork-sausage fair is held on the second Sunday in June. The town is also famous for its annual chestnut fair, which takes place on 18 and 19 October, and is bizarrely called the *foire aux chats* (cat fair) and not the *foire aux châtaignes*.

This quaint nomenclature reminds me of the most remarkable culinary experience of my life, which occurred as I was driving back from Jargeau to Orléans. You can take one of two routes, both pretty. South of the river the D951 passes through Sandillon, where a plaque on a former dairy-farm tells you that Joan of Arc's mother, Isabelle Romée, spent her declining years there waiting for her daughter's rehabilitation. The second takes you back across the bridge and then left through Mardié, with its pretty church and seventeenth-century canal locks.

On this latter route I once stopped by a good number of parked caravans belonging to Romanies. A young lad was blowing up what appeared to be very bristly balloons with a stirrup-pump. Then an older gypsy took his knife and speedily scraped away the bristles, leaving a pink puffed-up ball. I approached closer and discovered that these balloons were in fact dead hedgehogs. A fair number of live ones, recently caught, were crawling about at the bottom of a plastic dustbin. The Romany who was shaving the hedgehogs told me that he and his companions had caught enough that morning to feed the whole gipsy group. He kindly invited me to try the delicacy. I went with him to the table where the women had already cleaned and cooked some. The hedgehogs tasted like rather strong rabbit.

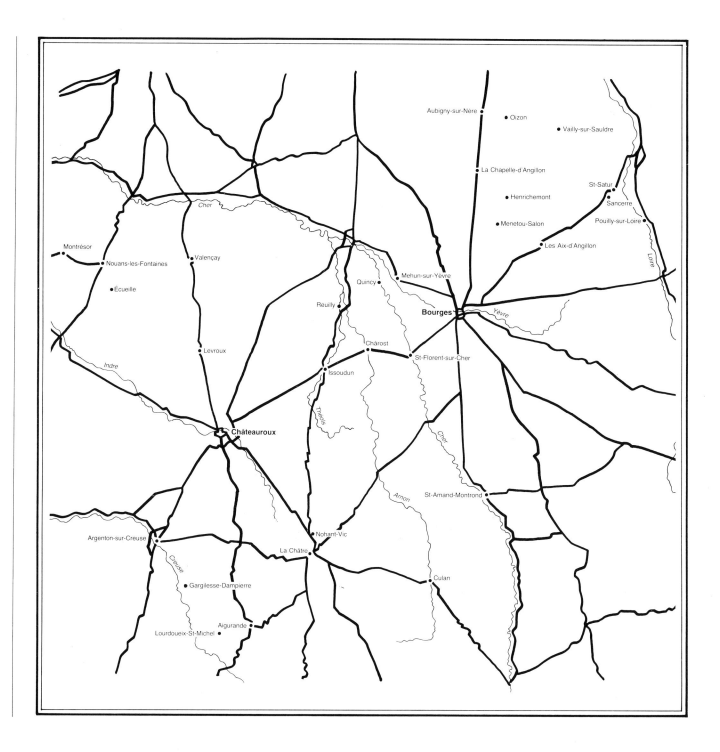

6
Flamboyance and Hidden Gems

Bourges – Sancerre – Aubigny-sur-Nère – La Chapelle-d'Angillon – Mehun-sur-Yèvre – Issoudun – Valençay – Levroux – Nohant-Vic

When that entertaining Edwardian traveller T. Frederick Bumpus visited Bourges, he found the railway journey south of Vierzon a great improvement on the French trains he had hitherto experienced. 'In this part of France,' he recorded, 'the long, open third-class carriages are far superior to those of the rabbit hutch kind with which I had become so familiar on the northern railways.' He was entranced when an old peasant woman with a couple of fowls in a basket put up an umbrella to shield them from the afternoon sun, 'an exquisite piece of drollery'. And then, about half-past two in the afternoon, he caught from the carriage 'the first glimpse of the great transeptless cathedral of Bourges rising at the summit of its city' and 'seen athwart a rich tract of pastoral country intersected by willow-bordered streams inviting a dip'. He made a mental note of the possibility of a dip, found a hotel and set off for a preliminary reconnoitre of the cathedral.

The following morning after breakfast he did manage an invigorating plunge in one of the willow-bordered streamlets, and then went to explore the magnificent building in earnest. He found himself, as every visitor must, 'perfectly overwhelmed with the breadth and majesty of this cathedral of Bourges'.

Bourges Cathedral, replacing an earlier romanesque basilica, was begun at the very end of the twelfth century by Archbishop Henri de Sully. Henri's brother Eudes was then Bishop of Paris, hence the plausible theory that Parisians from Notre-Dame worked on this masterpiece too. The work was finished within sixty years.

The building stands in the great tradition of French gothic cathedrals. Its west facade is brilliant – five stupendous portals topped by two quite different towers. The carved saints and angels on the portals seem to rush at each other head-first. The four doors flanking the great central portal depict scenes from the lives of the Virgin Mary, St William, St Stephen and St Ursinus. They pale beside the magnificent central depiction of Christ as the judge of all, flanked by the devil gorging himself on the damned and St Peter leading the saved to paradise. The towers are asymmetrical partly because that on the left fell down in 1506 and had to be rebuilt, and partly because the tower on the right was begun in the fourteenth century and has never been finished. The larger one is known as the butter tower (Tour de Beurre), since (it is said) cash was raised to rebuild it by granting donors indulgences to eat butter during Lent.

Walk around the south side of Bourges Cathedral for a feast of double flying buttresses, as if the architects simply had to build and build to shore the whole edifice up. These buttresses are in truth supporting five naves, the central one soaring to a height of over 40 metres. Perspectives multiply and vistas open out as you walk around the interior, with its immense yet (because of their height) seemingly slender pillars.

All the glass gleams, though in the clerestory windows the Old Testament prophets are placed on the north, darker side of the cathedral, since it was judged that they perceived only dimly what was to be revealed by Jesus's apostles, who are therefore portrayed in the much sunnier windows of the south side. Bourges Cathedral boasts altogether thirty rose windows. Above all, the glass of the choir chapels is marvellous, all of it made between 1215 and 1225. The windows depict the story of Joseph, the Apocalypse, the Last Judgment, St Thomas's mission to India, the passion of Christ, St John the Baptist, St John the

Above **The sweet smiles of the blessed: part of the Last Judgment carved over the west doorway of Bourges Cathedral.**

Left **The multiple perspectives of the vast interior of the cathedral of St Stephen, Bourges.**

monster, while outside they are tossed into a boiling cauldron.

Before leaving the cathedral find the chapel of Jacques Coeur, for its beautiful fifteenth-century glass: four windows, influenced if not made by Flemish masters, giving a continuous narrative of the nativity of Jesus. As you walk out of the cathedral, it is impossible not to pause before the splendid glass in the rose window of the west end, created in 1392.

Bourges sets off its cathedral well. Le Nôtre designed the beautiful garden to the south side in the seventeenth century, and the archbishops looked out on it until their palace, built in the same century, became the present town hall (Hôtel de Ville).

Below **The tremendous gothic Last Judgment sculpted on the west door of Bourges Cathedral. Above the door the dead are rising from their graves.**

Evangelist and St James the Great, and the saintly martyrs Lawrence, Vincent and Stephen (to whom this cathedral is dedicated). Other windows show the finding of St Stephen's relics and illustrate Jesus's parables of the Good Samaritan and of the rich man and poor Lazarus.

I find it fascinating to compare the Last Judgment illustrated here in stained glass (in the first window to the right in the aisle round the apse) with that carved on the west portal. The scenes and motifs are the same, the spirit totally different and yet equally brilliant. Here the damned are thrown into the jaws of a

Although T. Frederick Bumpus, standing in the garden one July afternoon, greatly admired its 'border of ageratum enclosing a medley of geraniums, roses, and heliotrope', this is not, in my view, the most entrancing garden in Bourges. That I judge to be one created in the twentieth century, the garden of the Prés-Fichaux in the boulevard de la République. The landscape gardener Paul Marguerita created it between 1923 and 1930 on the site of an old swamp. Its arched yew hedges are immensely appealing; its roses are delicate, their colours perfectly juxtaposed; its pools glitter with water-lilies.

From Le Nôtre's garden and the former archbishops' palace walk round the cathedral apse to the ancient tithe barn (the Grange aux Dîmes, No. 3 rue Molière), abutting onto the cathedral cloister. The Grange aux Dîmes is one of the oldest buildings in the city, put up in the thirteenth century to collect the taxes in kind levied by the cathedral chapter. The ground floor has pointed vaulting, and the upper storey is reached by a sweet, half-timbered external staircase.

From here Bourges offers clusters of delightful medieval and renaissance houses, in charming, often cobbled streets. Rue Molière leads to the gorgeous late gothic and renaissance Hôtel Lallemant, well worth a guided tour for its splendid vaulted kitchen and its charming oratory (mysteriously decorated on the ceiling with alchemists' symbols). The fact that Hôtel Lallemant is built on the old Gallo-Roman ramparts of Bourges explains why its two courtyards lie at different levels.

Walk on along rue Édouard-Branly to reach another fascinating piece of city architecture: the old Alderman's Hall (Hôtel des Échevins). Architecturally speaking, this building falls into two distinct parts. Half of it is fifteenth-century renaissance, including a lovely, flamboyantly decorated polygonal stair-turret; the other half – the classical arcaded gallery to the left, opening out onto the court – was built in the first half of the seventeenth century.

Just north of the Alderman's Hall is rue Mirabeau which, with the pedestrianized place Gordaine and rue Coursarlon, seems to me to boast timber-framed houses that top all the rest, with fantastic storeys overhanging the bars and tobacco shops that these medieval buildings have become at street level. A significant part of protestant history began here, for the great reformer John Calvin was educated at the Law School that still stands in rue Mirabeau, and from the pulpit that juts out into the street preached some of his first sermons.

A few paces to the north of rue Mirabeau you find the church of Notre-Dame, with its massive square bell-tower. This building, an entertaining mixture of fifteenth- and sixteenth-century styles, replaced an older one burned down in the terrible fire of 1487. Inside, the statue of a lady lying down in the south aisle represents the Blessed Jeanne de Valois, daughter of King Louis XI.

The hôtels of Bourges are by no means exhausted by what we have seen. The excellent sixteenth-century House of the Queen Blanche (No. 19 rue Gambon) lies to the west of the church of Notre-Dame. From here walk south through place Planchat and along rue des Arènes to see the pretty turrets of Hôtel Cujas, close by the city law court which was once an Ursuline convent (hence the seventeenth-century chapel next door, built as a Latin cross with a fine dome).

These noble houses speak of a rich commercial past. Hôtel Cujas, for example, bears specific witness to the historic trading importance of this city. As the ancient capital of the province of Berry, lying almost at the geographical heart of France, set on the Canal du Berry and where the Rivers Yèvre and Auron meet, Bourges attracted merchants from far and near. The Hôtel Cujas was built in 1515 by the architect Guillaume Pellevoysin for a wealthy Florentine merchant named Durando Salvi, who was established at Bourges. Its name derives from a later occupant, the once renowned teacher of Roman law, Jacques Cujas.

But for the most flamboyant example of mercantile success we must walk a few metres further along rue des Arènes to the famous Palais de Jacques-Coeur. Jacques Coeur was born at Bourges in the closing years of the fourteenth century. His father was a furrier. The son travelled as far as the Middle East, picking up financial skills wherever he went. His talents were rewarded when he was appointed steward of the finances and royal banker to Charles VII. He supervized the collection of revenues in the Languedoc for the Estates General and took charge of the notorious salt tax.

Soon Jacques Coeur's family was profiting from his financial genius and political manoeuvring. He managed to have his son Jean made Archbishop of Bourges. A brother became Bishop of Luçon. Jacques himself was knighted in 1441. He traded in wool and wheat, in salt and silk. His business emissaries ranged Scotland, Spain, Italy and Switzerland. The papacy granted him a dispensation to trade with the Muslim infidels of Alexandria. Coeur became rich enough to finance his own master, and his loans enabled Charles VII to recover Normandy from the English.

At Bourges he built the finest private house in France. The Palais de Jacques-Coeur was begun in 1443, utilizing two ancient towers of the Roman fortifications of the city. Part fortress, part finely decorated palace, to visit this beautiful building is to enter the rich world of a fifteenth-century merchant. Everywhere you come across the emblems of Jacques Coeur: hearts and scallop-shells, with his device proclaiming that nothing is impossible to valiant hearts ('A VAILLANS COUERS RIENS IMPOSSIBLE'). The owner's own luxurious taste is displayed in the monumental chimney and the ingenious kitchens. His financial skills are celebrated by motifs carved on the central one of three beautiful staircase turrets fronting the main courtyard. His genius for trade is displayed over one doorway inside the palace in a carved relief of a fully rigged merchant ship, rippling along the waves.

Coeur's culture and love of music appear in the painting of Tristan and Isolde in the treasury and in the minstrels' gallery of the dining hall. The skills of the architects unobtrusively support their patron's display, save where they suddenly reveal their own virtuosity in, for example, a superbly convoluted wooden ceiling.

Sadly Jacques Coeur did not end his days in this palace. Such men make enemies, and when the king's mistress Agnès Sorel died suddenly of dysentry, Coeur was accused of poisoning her. Imprisoned and savagely fined, he managed to escape to Florence and then to Rome, where he entered the service of the Pope. Callixtus III was at that time implacably at odds with the Turks, and in 1456 he sent Coeur to the Aegean to organize a naval sortie against them. There on 25 November he died.

After the cathedral, the Palais de Jacques-Coeur is the climax of any visit to Bourges. But one other church catches my fancy there, if only because of its odd name. South from the Palais de Jacques-Coeur along rue des Arènes stands the church of Saint-Pierre-le-Guillard, built in the mid thirteenth century (with side chapels, one containing the bones of Jacques Cujas, added 200 years later). The suffix 'le-Guillard' is said to derive from the name of a pious Jew, Zecharia Guillard, who paid for the church to be built. He had been converted to Christianity when his donkey spontaneously knelt before the Blessed Sacrament, which was being carried by St Antony of Padua on his visit to Bourges in 1225. This episode is illustrated inside the church, in painting and stained glass.

Bourges still prospers, partly today on the armaments industry that was established in the nineteenth century. If you think of eating here, do not hesitate to ask to sample the city's celebrated potato-cakes (*galettes de pomme de terre*). At Bourges and throughout the Berry country you can enjoy succulent *boulettes berrichonnes*, veal dumplings in a regional Berry sauce.

Bumpus said good-bye to Bourges Cathedral on a

Monday morning and left by train. In truth I would preferably neither arrive nor leave this great city by train. To explore the region around Bourges you must be prepared for slightly longer drives than those which revealed the treasures of the Loiret, even making the occasional zig-zag detour to see places as fascinating as La Chapelle-d'Angillon or Mehun-sur-Yèvre; but remarkable treasures still appear, and the railway train misses them.

The first such treasure is the partly fortified Les Aix-d'Angillon, reached by driving east from Bourges along the N151 and then turning left to drive northeast along the D955. Several times during the Hundred Years War the English destroyed most of Les Aix-d'Angillon. Each time the town rose again. Not surprisingly its two churches have both been considerably restored. But the older, twelfth-century building is not to be despised. The western facade was reconstructed in the nineteenth century, but the exterior of the apse is a splendidly playful piece of romanesque decoration. Inside and out the chancel is lovely, with carved columns and simple, satisfying embellishment. On either side of the high altar are eighteenth-century reliquary busts of two bearded and mitred bishops. The countryside around the small town is lovely. Les Aix-d'Angillon possesses a tree-shaded communal lake, with benches for the picnickers, where you can (with a permit) fish in season. You find it by making for the town cemetery and following the signs for the 'Étang'.

The D955 leads from here to Sancerre, rising like a Tuscan hill town, with red-tiled houses crawling up to its château. Half-way up the winding road by the ramparts you gain a stupendous panorama of the River Loire curling through gentle woodlands. Sancerre was

Sancerre, set on a hill in the distance, fortified and peaceful at the same time.

a powerful fortress of refuge during the Hundred Years War and the Wars of Religion. Today only the massive, cylindrical keep, the Tour des Fiefs, remains of its medieval château. The centre of the city, La Nouvelle Place, has been pedestrianized, with ungainly flights of steps. Walk from here down rue Saint-Jean as far as place du Beffroi to see the church of Notre-Dame and its splendid sixteenth-century bell-tower. Notre-Dame itself was begun in 1658 and much changed and restored over the centuries, so that the present building is virtually a late nineteenth-century church. Much of the furniture inside dates from the 1970s, and a fresh restoration of the exterior was begun in 1980.

Sancerre is a city of narrow streets, with numerous picturesque old houses and local craftsmen making and selling pottery. The countryside around Sancerre is rolling and varied, with hectares and hectares of vineyards. This region has been producing noted wines since the eleventh century. Today the whites, reds and rosé wines are made chiefly from the renowned Pinot and Sauvignon grapes. White Sancerre made from the Sauvignon grape was granted its *appellation contrôlée* in 1936; Sancerre red and rosé in 1959.

The white is fruity and nervous, grown on chalky soils, and generally drunk young. Some of it is matured in vast cellars created when stones were quarried for Bourges Cathedral, and where the temperature scarcely varies from one year to the next. Pouilly-sur-Loire just to the east of Sancerre produces a light white wine, that has a glint of emerald in its yellowish hue and leaves a delectably musty afterglow in the mouth. Pouilly-Fumé and Blanc-Fumé de Pouilly are white wines from this region with a lot of strength.

Southwest of Sancerre, just off the D940, the commune of Menetou-Salon offers a perfumed red that hints at the taste of strawberries, as well as extremely pleasant white wines and rosés. The poorer, sandy soil at Quincy still further southwest manages to grow another good dry white wine, while to the west at

Reuilly, in the neighbouring *département* of Indre, the vineyards nourish Pinot Noir grapes that will be pressed immediately after the harvest to produce a brisk and thirst-quenching rosé. Here too the famous Sauvignon grape produces fine white wines.

The best time for sampling these wines is the Whitsun weekend, at the great Sancerre wine fair. If you miss this fair, try the 'wine days' at Sancerre held on the fourth weekend of August. Otherwise, call at one of the vintners of Sancerre who invites you to taste for nothing (*dégustation gratuite*) before buying, or else visit the extensive cellars 'de la Mignonne' (open all the year round except for the month of January), just outside Sancerre on the way to Saint-Satur (the D955), where Augustinian monks were making renowned wines in the Middle Ages.

The viticolters of this region recommend drinking their white wines with fish and crabs and crayfish, as well as with the delicious goats' cheese that is made in Berry. The people of the Berry claim to breed the finest sheep in France, and at the hamlet of Chavignol they certainly produce a goats' cheese (known as *le crottin de Chavignol*) that has gained nationwide fame. Just outside Sancerre on the route de Bourges the Cooperative d'Élevage Caprin des Garennes invites you to taste for nothing (and then buy) cheeses made from the milk of over 300 goats.

From Sancerre you drive northwest along the D923 to reach a town to gladden the hearts of the Scots: Aubigny-sur-Nère. The road takes you through Vailly-sur-Sauldre, with its ruined fourteenth-century château, and then on by way of the beautiful château of La Verrerie at Oizon. Here is a hint of the Scottish connection, for this exquisite renaissance home, by a lake in the forest, was built by Béraud Stuart, and

---

Vines which produce the delicate, refreshing wines of Sancerre.

another Stuart, Robert, added an elegant loggia when he returned from the Italian wars in 1525. Their descendants sold the château to the Marquis de Vogüé in 1842. Still in private possession, it is open every day from March to the end of November.

Aubigny-sur-Nère proclaims itself the 'city of the Stuarts'. It gained the title during the Hundred Years War. The English sacked and burned the town in 1359. They took it again (and again set fire to it) in 1412.

Eight years later the dauphin appealed to the Scots for help against their traditional enemies, who were now occupying the greater part of France. The response of John Stuart of Darnley, Constable of the Scottish army, was to bring a great number of troops who materially contributed to the French victory at Baugé near Angers. Stuart was granted an annual pension of 2000 pounds (in the currency of Tours). The continuing war so stretched the finances of the French monarchy that the dauphin proved unable to keep up the payments. After his accession to the throne as Charles VII, instead of these annual payments he made over to John Stuart by letters patent of 23 March 1423 'the town, land, castle and wardship of Aubigny-sur-Nère'.

Aubigny-sur-Nère took John Stuart's coat of arms as its own – three buckles of gold on a background of purple – and preserves them to this day. The Scotsman continued to fight valiantly for the French. He lost an eye and was captured by the English at the battle of Crevant. After his release he made a pilgrimage to the Holy Land, returning to sacrifice his life at the battle of Harengs, near Orléans, in 1428.

The Stuart dynasty, basing itself at Aubigny-sur-Nère, proved firm allies of the French monarchy. For his services to Charles VIII and Louis XII in their Italian campaigns, Béraud Stuart was granted the extraordinary title, 'Chevalier sans reproche' – 'impeccable knight'. The other Stuart, Robert, fought with such distinction in the Italian campaigns of Louis XII and François I that he was made Marshal of France. And these fighting Stuarts had a material effect on their fief, Aubigny-sur-Nère. Like many a French soldier, they returned from Italy fired by Italian renaissance architecture.

An opportunity to rebuild the town occurred in 1512 when an immense fire ravaged virtually every building. This disaster would have ruined Aubigny-sur-Nère as the frightful fire of 1487 almost ruined Bourges, but for the largesse of Robert Stuart. He placed the trees of his seigneurial forest at the disposal of those who needed to rebuild – at a price, of course – and then used his profits from this generosity to further embellish his town and his château.

The château at Aubigny-sur-Nère is now the town hall. Robert Stuart began rebuilding an old fortress as

Detail from a sixteenth-century timbered house at Aubigny-sur-Nère, built when the town prospered under the Stuarts.

soon as the town became his fief, and the Stuart dynasty continued to embellish it. The pavilion-entrance, with its little turrets and tall chimney, far from repelling potential invaders, is positively welcoming, and you ought to walk through it to see the gardens laid out by Le Nôtre (or one of his disciples) in the seventeenth century. Scarcely anything of the medieval château survives (just as you find only three towers and a few metres of walls – along boulevard de la République – surviving from the formidable fourteenth-century ramparts that once surrounded the town).

Walk from the château down rue du Prieuré as far as the so-called house of François I and the house of Joan of Arc. The first is exceptionally fine, though some of the carved statues on the wooden beams have sadly deteriorated since the house was built in 1519. The statue on the corner post once represented St Martin of Tours, though no one would ever guess that today. The house of Joan of Arc, in rue des Dames, is so named because of its fine doorway which bears a likeness of the maid.

Down rue de l'Église you find the renaissance Maison du Bailli, another half-timbered house which even sports a wooden portrait medallion of Béraud Stuart himself, turning fiercely to the right, his long hair sternly falling to his shoulders, looking far more like an Italian renaissance prince than a Franco-Scottish war-lord.

Aubigny-sur-Nère's twisting medieval streets (rue de Bourg-Coutant, rue des Foulons, rue Cambournac, as well as the place Adrien Arnoux and the old market square) are a continual delight as each turn reveals another renaissance half-timbered house. Where a tiny bridge (the pont des Foulons) crosses the waters of the Nère is a house said to be the only one to survive the fire of 1512 intact.

The Nère is a stream that flows down from the hills around Sancerre and runs through Aubigny-sur-Nère before joining the River Sauldre. Rue des Foulons

Another superb detail from a sixteenth-century timbered house at Aubigny-sur-Nère.

means Fullers' Street, and the Nère for centuries drove mills where the wool of the sheep from Berry and the Sologne was carded (indeed, an alternative name for this town is still 'Aubigny-les-Cardeaux'). Louis XIV's finance minister Jean-Baptiste Colbert set up a woollen factory here in the seventeenth century. It was a draper named Pierre Bompain who brought the protestant faith in the sixteenth century. He had left his native town to avoid persecution – in vain. At Aubigny-sur-Nère the fiercely catholic John II Stuart implacably opposed the new Calvinist beliefs, arrested Bompain and delivered him to Paris, where he was executed. This act of persecution did little good for John II Stuart. He himself fell foul of the king and was imprisoned in 1546. He managed to make his peace at the accession of Henri II, fought with distinction in the royal armies and in 1562 was honoured by a visit of Charles IX to Aubigny-sur-Nère.

Nor did Bompain's execution halt the spread of protestantism here. By the end of the sixteenth century the town possessed two Calvinist pastors and one of only six protestant churches in Berry. Was it these Huguenots, I wonder, who mutilated the statue of St Martin of Tours on the house of François I?

Protestant weavers were renowned throughout France (and after their exile under Louis XIV they took many of their skills to England). Serge and cloth from Aubigny-sur-Nère brought wealth to the town. A reminder of those thriving times (when prosperity continued to be based on the cloth trade) can be seen in the town's seven annual fairs and its weekly markets. Today, however, its prosperity resides in the manufacture of electrical machinery, jewellery, gold and silverware, and in tourism (for Aubigny-sur-Nère has developed some good camping sites and as-siduously promotes fishing, hunting and such pursuits).

Prosperous towns build fine churches, and Aubigny-sur-Nère is no exception. The church of St Martin dates as far back as the twelfth century, but the devastation of the fire of 1512 means that today's church is a splendid gothic building, with later embellishments such as its flamboyant tower and early seventeenth-century stained glass, as well as some excellent classical stalls and statues. A great archway pierces its tower. Amidst all this grandeur I like the absurdly simple 1588 memorial on a pillar near the entrance, a crude carving of bones, a skull, and the cross of Lorraine.

The Stuart connection with Aubigny-sur-Nère received a boost in the second half of the seventeenth century when King Charles II of England claimed the town for his mistress Louise de Kéroualle. Born in a modest Breton manor house in 1649, Louise's social and political skills eventually made her Duchess of Portsmouth. The British parliament hated her, but she managed to remain secure in England until the Revolution of 1688. On her retirement to Aubigny-sur-Nère she chiefly displayed her charitable and religious instincts, endowing nuns, enlarging the château, seeking reductions in the taxes of the citizens of her town, looking after foundlings, the aged and the poor, and diverting part of the Nère when its noise kept her awake at night.

Her descendants, the Dukes of Richmond, fitfully kept up the British connection, but the Revolution and the subsequent Napoleonic war with Britain made their position intolerable. In 1812 their château at Aubigny-sur-Nère was auctioned off.

From Aubigny-sur-Nère drive directly south along the D940 to La Chapelle-d'Angillon. On 3 October 1866 the novelist Alain-Fournier was born at La Chapelle-d'Angillon, where his father was the local school-master. The most impressive sight as you first approach his birthplace is nothing to do with the novelist, but is the imposing towers of its moated château, first built in the eleventh century and rebuilt and enlarged from the fifteenth to the seventeenth. Apart from the ancient keep, all the rest – the chapel, the fine woodwork, staircase, monumental terrace, and vestiges of a renaissance rackets court – are embellishments of what was initially a mighty attempt to protect a tiny village from the marauding Normans. The village had grown up here in the first place around the tomb of St Jacques de Saxeau, who had fled to France to escape the iconoclasts of Constantinople.

Alain-Fournier, whose mother came from Aubigny-sur-Nère, was born in his parents' home, now No. 35, avénue Alain-Fournier. The discreet plaque placed on the wall of his birthplace in 1976, with the words:

Maison natale
d'Alain-Fournier
et de sa soeur
Isabelle

is already three-quarters covered in vine leaves. The novelist would probably not have minded. His masterpiece, *Le Grand Meaulnes*, evokes the lost happiness of his childhood here and describes what could easily be his own home (transformed into a secondary school at the edge of the village) as 'a long red building draped in Virginia creeper'.

Le Grand Meaulnes is a story of a romantic, mysterious, protective stranger, Augustin Meaulnes, and an idyllic love affair, set (as Alain-Fournier put it) 'in a remote manor house in wild and empty country'. By the time he published *Le Grand Meaulnes* in 1913 Alain-Fournier was already making a mark on the literary world, corresponding with and learning from his brother-in-law, the critic Jacques Rivière. He was also consumed with a nostalgic passion for the lost domains of his childhood, a passion expressed through the hero of his great novel. 'Meaulnes, big Meaulnes, the hero of my novel,' he told Jacques, 'is a man whose childhood was too beautiful. Throughout his whole adolescence it trailed after him.' At times it seems that this memory of paradise will overwhelm his whole life. Meaulnes comes to think that such a paradise can never be his again; and when one seems to offer itself, he flees in terror. Alain-Fournier was in part speaking of himself, and of a young and beautiful girl he himself had met in 1905. And this love that he had failed to grasp intensified his yearning for the long-gone joy he believed himself to have known as a child at La Chapelle-d'Angillon.

In 1914 Alain-Fournier went to war, leaving behind fragmentary chapters of a new novel, *Colombe Blanchet*. On 22 September he was killed in battle. He may have died crying 'Vive la France!'; he may not. Accounts differ. Alain-Fournier was his pen-name, a

At La Chapelle-d'Angillon the château is virtually impregnable across a vast stretch of water.

modification of his baptismal name, Henri Alban Fournier. In the tumbledown fifteenth-century church of La Chapelle-d'Angillon (which houses the ancient relics of St Jacques de Saxeau) the war memorial makes a valiant compromise, recording the death of 'Henri Alain Fournier' on 22 September 1914. This unsophisticated country war memorial is strangely touching, as if Alain-Fournier had somehow returned to his childhood paradise.

Eleven kilometres southeast of La Chapelle-d'Angillon (along the D12) lies the quaint village of Henrichemont. Sully rebuilt a little hamlet here in 1605 and named it after his master Henri IV ('Henrici Mons'). The village is basically a quadrilateral, around a pretty fountain. The rebuilding did not obliterate the villagers' ancient skills. There have been potters here since the twelfth century, and they still display their wares.

Drive back to Bourges by way of Mehun-sur-Yèvre, which you reach from Henrichemont by taking the D20 southwest. The church of Notre-Dame and the château at Mehun-sur-Yèvre stand in delicate juxtaposition to each other, close by gentle mills on the riverside. No one knows exactly when the church was founded: certainly by the mid eleventh century. The last aisle of the nave and the bell-tower were finished a hundred years later. In 1466 Raoul de Thierry added the chapel of the Virgin Mary, in a gothic style at odds yet not clashing with the romanesque church.

This was soon dubbed a seigneurial and royal chapel of the Dukes of Berry and Charles VII. The tourist might be slightly fazed by some oddities of restoration, necessary after the pillages of the Huguenots and a fierce fire of 1910, but the church well deserves its classification as one of the historic buildings of France. Devout seventeenth-century paintings by Jean Boucher – of the crucifixion and the 'betrothal' of Joan of Arc – enhance the interior, whose nave is a vast rectangle, $32\frac{1}{2}$ metres long, $10\frac{1}{2}$ metres wide and 13 metres high. A wall-painting by Grandin, dated 1886,

depicts the maid of Orléans consecrating her sword to Our Lady. In the baptistery chapel is a modern statue of St Joan, made of painted wood by François Brochet in 1955. She wears curious knee-breeches, reminiscent (to an Englishman, whatever they signify to the French) of a pantomime principal boy.

Joan of Arc was ennobled at Mehun-sur-Yèvre on 29 December 1429. Walk from the church across the square to the château, today little more than noble, battered towers and the remnants of a moat. Here Charles VII heard of the death of Charles VI on 20 October 1422. Here he chose to be proclaimed king in the church of Notre-Dame. Here on 22 July 1461 he died.

The road leads southeast from Mehun-sur-Yèvre to Bourges. South and west of the city are some little-known delights and several renowned and still entrancing places. Saint-Florent-sur-Cher (southwest of Bourges along the N151) is one of the former. Today its château is the town hall (Hôtel de Ville), a gentle sort of fortress, with irregular turrets, the perfect background for the Thursday market.

Then drive on to cross the River Arnon at Chârost (with its pretty pink stone church), to leave the *département* of Cher and enter the *département* of Indre. At Chârost a far-seeing eighteenth-century seigneur saw the Revolution coming and speedily divested himself of his privileges. The Revolution came all the same.

Now the *département* of Indre is crossed by the route N20 which, as M. Gilbert Mandard, sometime secretary of tourism for the region, once conceded, is 'not particularly attractive'. Most Frenchmen, he

---

The château at Mehun-sur-Yèvre, which was magically depicted in the famous *Très Riches Heures du duc de Berry*, **is still an imposing ruin, dominating the village made famous by Charles VII and Joan of Arc.**

Trees shade the River Indre which on a lazy summer afternoon seems almost still.

observed, speed along it in a headlong rush towards Spain and the sun. If, as he needed to insist to his fellow-countrymen, the Indre is an ideal region for 'le tourisme de weekend', much more does this delightful *département* need commending to visitors from other lands. An integral part of ancient Berry, this region is in truth filled with historical fascination, astonishing churches, fine châteaux and a thousand and one other delights. To find them you need to drive scarcely 10 kilometres off the beaten track. It is the land where Balzac wrote, Talleyrand held court, and George Sand loved and then rejected Chopin.

One reason for the comparative neglect of this *département* in recent times is that it seemed to be declining economically. Its population was decreasing and ageing, its old way of life stagnating. Yet the same phenomena produce a region rich in nostalgia and help

to preserve what modernization might otherwise destroy. To summarize the most recent arguments of those now responsible for this beautiful and unduly neglected part of France: swamps need protecting as well as sometimes draining; rationalization of farming can so alter the ecology of a region as to make it uninhabitable by some of our most vulnerable animals, birds and plants; and before we dredge or drain a single river, we ought to consider the consequences.

Tourists do not dredge rivers, though they may camp by them. Some tourists relish swamps and nature reserves. Most of us respond to history, architecture and good food. Opening up the *département* to tourism is one of the least destructive ways of aiding its economy.

Balzac wrote close to the town of Issoudun, a few kilometres southwest of Chârost. Issoudun, celebrated

A bridge spans the River Théols near the old priory at Issoudun.

locally for its red and rosé wines, seems to have been thriving since the Gauls lived here. Richard the Lionheart and Philippe Auguste fought over the town, each strengthening its fortifications. In 1200 Issoudun became royal property as part of the dowry of Blanche de Castile, and the monarchy granted the town the right to hold seven fairs a year (a privilege still exploited). Wisely, the citizens continued to strengthen the town walls and extend their château, though all that remains of it today is a powerful keep, built in 1202, and worth a visit solely to see its splendidly vaulted interior. In 1562 Issoudun was strong enough to keep out the troops of the Huguenots.

At Issoudun do not be put off by the dry-as-dust connotations of the word 'museum'. Signs directing visitors to the 'Musée' take you south of the town round the fortified wall, with little slits for shooting arrows through and the great tower. Water from the River Théols, crossed by a lovely two-arched bridge, runs underneath precarious houses. Then you reach the so-called 'Musée', in fact the delightful former monastery and hospice of St Roch. There is a twentieth-century museum/art gallery attached to the hospice, imaginatively run, with a new exhibition every two months. But this is not the main reason for coming.

The canons of Saint-Cyr at Issoudun founded a monastery/hospice here as early as the year 1144. Later it was run by a lay rector and sisters. Today the former monastic and hospital buildings constitute an absolutely charming ensemble dating from the fifteenth to the eighteenth centuries. The monks' quarters open onto a balcony overlooking a still cultivated garden of medicinal herbs.

At the heart of the whole complex lies its chapel, built around the year 1500 and adjacent to the room in which the sick men lay – especially those with dangerously contagious diseases. (Women patients were segregated from the men in a room under the monastic quarters, where the beds, still there, were

The ancestors of Jesus perch nonchalantly in the Jesse tree at Issoudun.

curtained to give a measure of privacy.) A door between the chapel and the men's sick bay would normally be closed, as would the shuttered window, which allowed these invalids to watch the celebration of the Mass and even to receive Holy Communion through the hole without, it was thought, coming too close to the healthy. Were the little drawings close by these windows done by the sick themselves?

The chapel itself contains two remarkable Jesse trees, that is to say genealogical tables of the ancestors of Jesus literally carved in the form of trees, with the alleged ancestors perched on the branches. The delicacy of the work is partly due to the local stone from which these Jesse trees were cut, for it is soft when quarried and hardens only when exposed to the open air. Two trees were needed (evidently oaks, since

they are carved with acorns) in order to show Jesus's royal and his religious ancestry. On the left his prophetic ancestors are carved. On the right he is depicted as the descendant of kings. The figure of Jesus has disappeared, though a symbolic Pelican remains (the bird supposed to represent Jesus by sacrificing its own flesh to feed its young). The kings and prophets are animated, beautifully clothed figures, kneeling to worship their Lord, save for David who stands facing us.

Two other sovereigns worship the King of kings in this chapel, namely Charlemagne and Louis IX, portrayed in lovely sixteenth-century stained glass. And on one Jesse tree is a beautiful carving of the Virgin Mary – in flames. The allusion is, I think, to the bush which Moses saw burning but not consumed. Mary, bearing the blazing light of the world, similarly proclaims the divinity and yet is not consumed by it.

In the courtyard and pharmacy garden a twisting staircase leads to a room containing Balzac's writing-table and a picture of one of his friends, Mme Zulma Carraud, who lived nearby in Château Frapesle. (Balzac wrote *La Rabouilleuse* (*A Bachelor's Establishment*) in her château.) Here too are pictures of the first mayor of Issoudun (appointed in 1798) and his family – usually, one might judge, portraits no one would exult over, save that the very headdresses that the ladies wear in their portrait are preserved at Issoudun.

In 1646 a pharmacy was built for the hospice and an apothecary appointed, to be fed, clothed and lodged here. The next rooms constitute a perfectly preserved seventeenth- and eighteenth-century pharmacy: great enamel jars labelled with different drugs and medicines; snakes in bottles; beautifully painted

Beautifully glazed medicine jars, each labelled with their contents (note the sixth jar from the left, second row up, for 'Expurgation') in the ancient pharmacy at Issoudun.

medicine boxes; phials of mercury; huge pestles and mortars and little ones too; massive scales; countless jugs and jars ranged in specially constructed cupboards around the walls; a library of old medical books; medical recipes (some of them made up of over seventy ingredients) from a hospice run by Sisters of Mercy at Reuilly; and a primitive but clearly effective still, made of hammered copper, for distilling all manner of potent remedies.

This is the oldest existing pharmacy in the whole region and is filled with rare and curious treasures. A group of glass jars is labelled with barely decipherable pieces of paper inscribed 'Dragon's blood', 'Crayfish eyes', 'Powdered goat's blood', 'Bone powder', and 'Zedoary' (i.e. the aromatic root of a plant grown in the East Indies). Tables of old surgical instruments make all but the most hardened medics shudder. In addition to these treasures the museum contains a series of parchments, the oldest being a letter from Pope Honorius III, the latest from the reign of Louis XV (some signed by the king himself), granting various rights to the hospice and its inhabitants.

Depending on how far you wish to drive now, a choice offers itself: a longer route to the delightful village of Levroux, taking in a couple of châteaux (including Valençay) on the way, or a shorter route, omitting the châteaux and driving directly to Levroux.

To visit Valençay, one of the most elaborate renaissance châteaux in the Loire valley, drive northwest from Issoudun along the D960. It opens to the public from Palm Sunday to All Saints' Day. Jacques d'Estampes began building the château at Valençay in 1540, inspired by Château Chambord (see p. 131). The whole sumptuous edifice was not finished until the seventeenth century. This is where Napoleon's foreign minister Talleyrand died in 1838 (having lived here since 1803), and most of the interior is decorated in the elaborate style of the First Empire.

Valençay can be overpowering. A charming antidote is to drive west (along the D960 and the D760)

Left **Valençay, begun in 1540 by Jacques d'Estampes, has a massive central keep inspired by the château at Chambord, though by the time the builders reached the end of the east wing, pepperpot towers had been superseded by vast classical domes. The smaller west wing was added in the seventeenth century. Here in the early nineteenth century Talleyrand lavishly entertained foreign ambassadors. Note the chimney piercing the eastern dome.**

Below **At Montrésor, where the River Indrois meets the River Olivet, Imbert de Bastarnay decided to abandon the dour old keep which he had inherited and built instead this delightful château, with its renaissance dormer windows flanked by pretty round towers.**

Below right **A peaceful street in the picturesque town of Montrésor, leading to the former collegiate church of St John the Baptist.**

through Nouans-les-Fontaines to the far less pretentious château at Montrésor. This picturesque little village, situated where the River Indrois meets the River Olivet, boasts a number of pretty ancient houses, and a gentle renaissance château built on a cliff by Imbert de Bastarnay in the sixteenth century. On display in the château are some fascinating Polish mementoes and works of art, left here by Count Branicki who restored the building in the nineteenth century.

We have slipped over into the *département* of Indre-et-Loire. To return to Indre a picturesque country route runs southeast from Nouans-les-Fontaines through Écueillé to Levroux. A shorter drive (avoiding the two châteaux of Valençay and Montrésor) would be to take the road south from Issoudun, turning almost immediately right on to the D8 to discover the totally unexpected delights of Levroux.

This little town takes its name from a leper (*lévreux*) healed here by St Martin of Tours in the fourth

201

century. As you approach from Issoudun, the ruined remains of the medieval château lie hidden by an obtrusive water-tower. The belfry and two west spires of the church dominate the town. You reach the church by going through the fortified town gate (built between 1435 and 1506) and along the main street to place Victor-Hugo, which also houses a fifteenth-century wooden house. This is the 'Maison de Jacques', so called because it sheltered pilgrims on their way to the shrine of St James at Compostela in Spain. Three bizarre men are carved on one of the thick wooden pillars of this house, one with a goat's head, the other with a sheep's head, the third covered completely in leprous scales.

Levroux church is dedicated to St Sylvain — allegedly the same person as the tax-collector Zachaeus whom Jesus called as a disciple. Legend insists that this Zachaeus evangelized Gaul and built a church here when Levroux was called Gabatum. In this church he was eventually buried. According to the famous and untrustworthy history of St Gregory of Tours, St Martin was coming to pray over the tomb of St Sylvain when he healed the leper. Whatever the truth of these tales, you can still see the skull of Sylvain at Levroux (in the chapel to the left of the high altar), accompanied by ex voto tablets thanking him for miraculous favours. One of the stained-glass windows inside the church (the first one on the right) illustrates an entertaining miracle performed by Sylvain while he was still alive. It tells the story of a young girl named Rhodène who was converted by the saint's preaching and asked for baptism. She decided to become a nun.

At La Corroirie near Montrésor even this simple domestic scene reveals centuries of architectural development, for the house on the left, with its jolly renaissance dormer window, stands next to far more ancient farm buildings.

When her fiancé Corrusculus arrived, she savagely mutilated her face, to put him off marriage. St Sylvain would have none of this. He miraculously restored her beauty, at which Corrusculus cried 'I shall not touch her again.' He too asked for baptism, and Rhodène became not his bride but his godmother. She founded her own monastery and built a fountain whose waters in later years healed innumerable diseases.

The Wars of Religion damaged some of the fine thirteenth-century carvings on the outside of the church, though over the west door you can still decipher people depicted opening their own coffins and climbing out at the general resurrection of the dead. The horseshoe nailed over the door dates from the same religious wars, when a farrier set up business in part of the church – a shop not closed down till 1852. Before going into the church, walk round to the south porch, where twenty-one carved faces grimace with emotion.

Inside, the thirteenth-century nave is soaring and beautiful. It houses a remarkable collection of artistic treasures. In the baptistery chapel on the left, for instance, hangs a fifteenth-century representation of the Trinity – a great rarity because the Council of Trent in the sixteenth century forbade such images as likely to give a false notion of the relationship between the three divine persons, and most of them were destroyed or otherwise mutilated. Here God the Father wears a papal tiara, and the Holy Spirit is a dove flying down to succour the crucified Son.

Just round the corner on the west wall is a statue of the same date depicting St James as a pilgrim, himself on his way to Compostela, a cockleshell on his hat. From a roof boss over the high altar a beautifully carved God the Father blesses us. This apparently obscure church possesses one of the three remaining gothic organ-cases in Europe (the other two being at Strasbourg and at Le Monastier in the Upper Loire). This organ-case dates from the end of the fifteenth century, as do the superb wooden choir stalls, whose

Left A cottage by the River Creuse.

Below The vast abbey at Fontgombault, on the western tip of the *département* of Indre, 82 metres long, 30 metres wide and 18 metres high, is one of the best preserved romanesque and fourteenth-century abbeys in France, and well worth a detour west from Argenton-sur-Creuse.

fifty-two misericords depict virtues and vices, animals and fools. Is the influence of pilgrimages to Compostela in Spain visible in the turbanned head of a Moor?

The craftsman responsible for these stalls was called Jean Cœur and he too was responsible for the flamboyant gothic chapel of the Blessed Virgin (the second chapel on the right). A melancholy memento in the shape of a heart records that François de Fiesque, Lord of Levroux, died at the siege of Montauban in 1621. His body was buried there. His heart was brought back home.

The first chapel on the right still preserves some of its thirteenth-century colouring. It also contains a surprising treasure (if that is the correct word), a late nineteenth-century stained-glass window signed by Luc-Oliver Merson, who made the famous mosaic inside the basilica of Sacré-Cœur in Paris. It represents Jesus revealing his sacred heart to St Margaret Mary Alocoque, who looks up from a garden filled with enormous artichokes.

Levroux is virtually due north of Châteauroux, a drably industrialized place possibly just redeemed by some pleasant renaissance and gothic houses and the church of Saint-Martial. A bypass will take you on to Argenton-sur-Creuse. The vast château with its splendid panoramas was taken by Henri IV in 1589 and deliberately ruined on the orders of Cardinal Richelieu in 1632. In that year the town was saved from the great plague that savaged most of Europe, after the people had begged the aid of the Virgin Mary. Since that time they make an annual procession to give thanks at the foot of her statue, which today is an enormous gilded nineteenth-century giantess, blessing the town.

From here you can explore the country of George Sand. Because of her many lovers and her diatribes against the constraints of marriage, some have called her the first liberated woman. But she also was entranced by what she regarded as the simplicity and charm of the rustic life. Even her masculine name was as much a bucolic device as an aggressive attack on a masculine establishment, for 'George' is the common nickname of a man from Berry.

The narrator of her novel *Jeanne*, published in 1844, begins resolutely, 'I am a man of the people,' and then proceeds to tell the tale of a country girl, as glorious as Joan of Arc, who lived and died unknown. *Les Maîtres sonneurs* (*The Bag-Pipers*), written in 1853, proclaims the author's Rousseauesque belief that 'the peasantry guess or comprehend far more than people think them capable of understanding'. *La Petite Fadette* was written five years earlier, during the convulsions of the revolution of 1848, with the intention, she wrote, of 'preaching unity to men who are viciously at one anothers' throats'. *La Mare au diable* (*The Devil's Pool*) sets out what she described as 'the beauty of simplicity' among those who live 'far distant from the corrupted life of great cities', i.e. in her own part of the Loire valley.

True, the pastoral tales, in which hemp-dressers tell naive yet profound tales after work, also depict men and women successfully loving each other in spite of society's disapproval. In *The Devil's Pool* a girl of sixteen marries a man aged twenty-eight and everyone dances, feasts and sings all night long, the old men of the village recovering neither their wits nor their legs until dawn. The hero and heroine of *François le champi* (*François the Waif*), after the suffering that inevitably accompanies romantic love, marry and live in idyllic happiness. ('Is the story true?' asks a listener at the end. 'If it is not, it might be,' answers the hemp-dresser.) Love redeems and transforms, George Sand avers, even love which many would count as illicit. In one tale Bernard Mauprat, a young savage, falls almost

---

Argenton-sur-Creuse is divided by the blue waters of the River Creuse. Note the seventeenth-century bridge in the distance, and the massive buttresses of the old priory church on the left.

Above **Aimé Millet's statue of George Sand (musing, no doubt, over one of her own novels of regional life) at La Châtre.**

incestuously in love with his cousin Edmée. The untameable is tamed. The unconquerable strength of womanhood, expressed through true love, changes the brute into a man.

The connection between George Sand's rustic romanticism and her avant-garde attitude to love and marriage is clear in these novels. Deep and pure emotions come before intellect. As she observes in *The Devil's Pool*, even the countryman sentenced to a life of endless, uncultivated toil 'is nobler than the man in whom knowledge has stifled feeling'. Such views, whatever their impact now, made an extraordinary impression on her contemporaries. John Stuart Mill declared that her writings 'act upon the nervous system like a symphony of Haydn or Mozart'.

Two of her most celebrated works were *Journal de Gargilesse* (*Diary of Gargilesse*) and her *Promenades autour d'un Village* (*Promenades around a Village*), both written about Gargilesse-Dampierre where she had a home. Gargilesse-Dampierre is an exquisite village, built in what is almost a ravine by the side of the River Creuse. (You reach it by taking the D48 and then the D40 south from Argenton-sur-Creuse.) Every wall is

Below **The artists' village of Gargilesse-Dampierre, where George Sand would visit her friend Marceau and where she eventually bought a house. Note the powerful twelfth-century tower of the church of Notre-Dame.**

Right **Just south of Gargilesse-Dampierre is Cuzion, whose village church of Saint-Stephen was built in the twelfth century when such buildings were often strongly fortified, in case the villagers needed shelter from marauders.**

The massive twelfth-century church at Lourdoueix-Saint-Michel, fortified for fear of protestant attacks during the Wars of Religion.

ivy clad, with many flowers set out in boxes. Narrow winding streets lead up to the romanesque church, carved on the outside with the customary wild men and bizarre beasts. Inside, even more bizarrely, a fresco over the high altar depicts the Virgin Mary, herself bearing the marks of the passion – nails, pincers, the ladder of the deposition – instead of her son. Other steep, narrow streets lead down to the altogether charming Maison George Sand.

George Sand's principal home in the Loire valley was Château Nohant, at Nohant-Vic, northeast of Gargilesse-Dampierre on the D943. An enjoyable route is to take the D40 and then D36 south and east through Lourdoueix-Saint-Michel (with its fifteenth-century château and a twelfth-century church that was

fortified against protestant attacks in 1445) as far as Aigurande, which boasts a lovely church dedicated to Our Lady, built in the eleventh century and beautifully embellished over the next 700 years. Then drive northeast until the D951 joins the D940, where you turn left and drive as far as La Châtre. The old quarter of this sweet town preserves some entrancing fifteenth- and sixteenth-century houses, a gothic well, splendid classical hôtels of the seventeenth and eighteenth centuries, a sixteenth-century Carmelite monastery (now the town hall) and a statue of George Sand herself (by Aimé Millet) – all guarded by the fifteenth-century château. In its keep now is a museum dedicated to George Sand, as well as a collection of stuffed birds.

From La Châtre the D943 takes you directly to Nohant-Vic. The sleepy countryside here is ideal for picnics, disturbed only by sheep and white heifers. Château Nohant is situated in a gorgeous little village just off the main road. A restaurant faces the village square, which embraces a church built in the twelfth and thirteenth centuries. The wooden lean-to porch to the church is said to be even older.

In 1836 George Sand had met Chopin in Paris and fallen in love with him. Two years later she had overcome his scruples and fear of public censure and had lured him to Nohant. From Nohant she took him to Majorca in a vain attempt to save his precious health. They were expelled from their villa there when the owner learned of the composer's tuberculosis. Chopin spent an idyllic summer in 1839 recovering at Nohant. Each summer he would return, mothered by the liberated mistress of the château, producing both miniatures and major works here. Eventually they

At Culan, east of La Châtre, this fierce château was founded on a cliff in the twelfth century and made even more fearsome in the fifteenth.

quarrelled. After 1848 Chopin never returned to Nohant. The following year he was dead.

Chopin is buried in the cemetery of Père Lachaise, Paris. George Sand was for a time devastated by his death, believing that her continued care might have saved him – even though, as she declared in her novel *Jacques*, 'I have never imposed constancy on myself, and always when I felt that love was dead and Providence leading me elsewhere, I acknowledged this without remorse.' She continued to write, publishing an autobiography and (three years before her death in 1876) some charming tales for her grandchildren. At Nohant-Vic you can visit both her château and her grave.

The route back to Bourges might well take in the splendid château built on an escarpment over the River Arnon at Culan (which you find by taking the D943 southeast from Nohant-Vic to La Châtre and then following the same road east). From here drive north to Saint-Amand-Montrond, which is really two medieval towns joined in one, and where there is another delightful château.

From Saint-Amand-Montrond the N144 is an easy road back to Bourges, the prefecture of Cher. Is there time en route to turn off the main highway and discover another entrancing, virtually unknown spot in the Loire valley? There are many. But it is time to remember a lament of George Sand after the success of her first bucolic novel:

'This little nook of Berry, this unknown *Vallée Noire*, this quiet and unpretentious landscape, which needs to be sought out and loves to be admired, was the sanctuary of my first and last dreams. For twenty-two years I had lived among the pollarded trees, these rutted roads, and beside these tangled thickets and these streams whose banks allow the passage only of children and sheep. All of it had charms for me alone and did not deserve to be revealed to the idly curious. Why betray the incognito of this modest countryside?'

At Ainay-le-Vieil, just south of Saint-Amand-Montrond, you can just see the renaissance part (with its chimney) behind the threatening moated walls of the medieval château.

Index